THE MOSCOW METHOD

HOW TO SELL YOURSELF WITHOUT SELLING

by

Dexter Moscow

Dear Nisha,

I hope you find The Book interesting

[signature]

1

Parvus Magna Press

102 Manachester Drive, Leigh on Sea, Essex, SS9 3EZ

Email: sharif@pmpress..co.uk

Website: www.pmpress.co.uk

FIRST EDITION – February 2018

British Library Cataloguing in Publication Data. A catalogue record and a copy of this book are available from the British Library

ISBN: 978-1-910372-21-0

Parvus Magna Press publishes Business and Educational books in the UK. If you would like to see your book in print, please email your manuscript to sharif@pmpress.co.uk

This book is dedicated to

My darling wife Fran, who has lived this book with me.

My son Alex, who challenged me.

His twin brother Elliot, who advised me.

Ella, Jack, Maddie and Maisie, my Grandkids; now you know what Papa does.

THE PURPOSE OF THIS BOOK

To offer a practical self help guide to those who want to excel at business pitching, presenting and speech making and who seek to get their ideas, products or services to a wider audience.

To be influential and engage with power and impact be it to an audience of one or many at the front of the room, around a boardroom table, at a networking meeting or a social function.

Contents

Introduction

REALITY CHECK – PEOPLE HATE BEING SOLD TO

In today's highly competitive world it is becoming increasingly difficult to get your voice heard over the noise generated by your competitors.

How do you differentiate your proposition, product or service to that of your competitors? Is there really such as thing as a unique selling point? I believe not. The only true differentiation is you.

Unlike in America where being a sales person is a noble profession. In the UK we regard sales people with mistrust and suspicion. Look at TV programmes like 'FAKE BRITAIN'; they constantly warn us about fraudsters and counterfeiters who promise much and deliver second rate goods and services.

There is an old adage that states 'if it looks too good to be true, then it probably is'.

Which poses a question; how do you prevent yourself becoming invisible amongst the torrent of information being fed to consumers and your target market?

Mobile phones, YouTube, Facebook, Twitter, LinkedIn and a myriad of other media outlets are the main source of the public's information and you need to be a part of that. Online sales have gone through the roof, because internet consumers are more clued in, informed and discerning than at any other time in the history of selling.

It is a tough market out there, generating new leads is tough, getting in front of prospects is tough, 'selling' to them once you are in front of them is tough.

Your competition is, in the main, saying the same thing as you are.

There are never enough hours in the day for you to complete your tasks, so how do you expect your prospects to have time to read your emails, scan your marketing materials, listen to your podcasts or view your YouTube clips?

You need to find another way.

If you're anything like me you are fed up with being pitched to at networking events, angry at being harassed by cold calls or aggravated by sales people assuming they know what is best for me. So if you feel like that, what do you think your prospects, clients and colleagues feel?

The old sales methods of pre-empted closes, aggression and pushiness and never answering questions directly don't work anymore. Pitching or presenting using PowerPoint and 'look books' are boring and yesterday's technology.

The internet has radically changed how we buy, access information and make decisions. You need to find a new, more consultative approach; a process that enables you to find out what your prospects real needs are.

Today's reality is that it is no longer enough for you to be technically brilliant at what you do, you need to be able to present yourself as dynamic, engaging and genuinely interested in how to resolve other people's problems.

You need to maximise your time and effort in front of your prospects who are, in reality, suspects. They are suspicious of you until you have developed a position of trust, and they feel that you fully understand their situation.

You need to find new ways of conveying information, rather than relying on emails, your website or direct mail. You need to be persuasive, powerful, a thought leader in your sector, a perceived expert in your field and, even more importantly, you need to enlighten, entertain and enthral, knowing which 'hot spots' to hit.

In short, you need to create a platform to win more business.

The key to your personal and financial success is in your ability to positively influence others to be delighted to take the action you desire them to take.

Why go live?

The pendulum is swinging back and it is no longer enough to communicate by email, through social media or written marketing material. Statistics show that increasingly people prefer 'in person' communication at live events, via webinars, at conferences, symposiums and breakfast networking events.

It is considerably easier to engage with people in these environments where the specific purpose of attending is to connect with others and create relationships. As Richard Branson said in a recent blog "No matter how advanced our methods of communication have become, nothing seems to have come close to replicating the value of face to face contact." He offers further statistical evidence in an infographic that can be accessed here:

http://bit.do/DMF2F

A Word of Caution

Over more years than I care to say, I have spent a fortune attending networking events, conferences and symposiums. Wasted hours of my valuable time conducting 1-2-1s with people who are never going to do business with me, or refer me to others.

I've drunk a tsunami of coffee, tea and diet coke and sat through endless power point presentations bored out of my mind.

I don't want you to make the same mistakes I've made, so rather than work the room why not command it? Take the opportunity to present to a room of prospects and get them to flock to you.

In today's challenging business environment, if you are not taking the advantage by presenting your products, services or ideas at the myriad of networking and business meetings that happen every day at all hours of the day and night, you are missing a golden opportunity to talk about your proposition in greater depth.

Don't spend your precious time and money meeting people 1-2-1, when you could literally take centre stage and present to a larger audience, tell your story and gain larger and more lucrative contracts.

In a recent Harvard Business Review it states that face-to-face meetings are still the most effective way to get your message across, generate leads and sell your ideas. By getting people to come to you, you can qualify them and then decide whether to take it to the next stage.

When coaching sales professionals, I am always told "if I can get in front of them I can get them on my side".

Why is this the case? Because people buy people first. When you connect with a person on an emotional level, trust is created and they will at least give you an opportunity to pitch what you're selling.

David Sandler of the Sandler Sales Institute said that "people buy emotionally, decide logically". Your job is to firstly offer an emotionally compelling reason to do business with you.

The problem, of course, is getting in front of them in the first place. It's therefore not surprising that conferences are coming back in fashion and people are realising that speaking at conferences, at networking events and at exhibitions is an excellent way to generate leads, gain interest and create engagement.

The key is ensuring that those engagements turn into opportunities to meet.

I hear you say "Yes, but it doesn't always work out like that". So why is that?

Why is it that some people receive acclaim for their presentations, gain major contracts and repeat business, while others miss the opportunity, do not get the results they want or never get invited back?

For me, one of the essential keys behind a business-winning presentation, compared with one that fails, is to understand people hate being sold to; they prefer to be informed. Therefore, you need to find a way *to sell without selling*.

Why read this book?

We live in an age of sound-bite selling and instant gratification, where our attention span is that of a goldfish and our recall of information is about the same. So how do people like Donald Trump, Nigel Farage, Simon Cowell, and Tony Blair manipulate and move us to take the action they desire us to?

You may not agree with what they say, but you should not ignore how they say it, and the effect it has on their audiences. Key features are repetition of key points, relevant personal stories and emotionally connecting words and phrases.

Taking the principles, processes and experiences of my previous careers, I have developed a number of empirically proven frameworks, used by major organisations and owner-run businesses to develop their selling and presenting skills. Let me share those business winning processes with you to put those same keys in your hands.

The first step to your success is to understand these abiding principles: -

- Look right
- Sound right
- Use the right phrases
- Understand what your audience wants

If not, you might as well whistle in the wind.

So often, I have heard business pitches and presentations of excellent content but they fail to win business. Why? Because the speaker has been unable to reach out and touch the consciousness and emotions of their audience.

In this book I will walk you through step-by-step guides of how to impress and motivate an audience of one or of many. We'll start from the moment before you open your mouth, through to when you close it.

After a long career developing selling propositions and business presentations, I've come to a realisation that, when considering how to improve our personal impact and influence, there are universal principles. When these are adhered to they can transform the average sales presentation into one that is engaging, persuasive and compels people to take the action you want them to take.

These principles are not specific to any sector, personality type or presentation style. Having worked across a wide range of industries and with people from every level of business, I've found they consistently deliver incredible results.

I have also studied the great orators of our time and analysed their vocal tricks, use of language, body positioning, emotional devices and the 'convincer strategies'. They use these to sell their ideas, propositions and concepts and they work regardless of their subject and their audience.

I will share these principles with you, along with client case studies from the individuals, major organisations and client companies I have worked with and the results of my analysis of legendary speakers.

They include Martin Luther King, Winston Churchill, John F Kennedy, Jay Zee, and Dr Joseph Lowery, who delivered the Inauguration Benediction for Barack Obama (more of him later).

These processes are not theoretical, but tried and tested systems that I use on a daily basis to achieve positive results, win high-level contracts and gain referrals from my talks. They are techniques that I coach others to use to gain buy-in from colleagues, customers, clients, stakeholders and their boards of directors.

A great presentation does not just happen. It should follow a specific framework enabling you to prepare effectively, develop compelling content and deliver that content with power and impact. It has to have a dynamic, clear and specific message that engages us at a deep psychological level.

I hope you enjoy the journey we'll take together.

Chapter 1

HOW TO SELL WITHOUT SELLING

"30 seconds to air".

"Dex, you'll be on camera 3".

The disembodied voice came down my earpiece and I checked once again that the impressive TASCO telescope was in place and all the lenses were ready to demonstrate. I looked over to Rob Locke, my co-presenter, who gave me the thumbs up to go ahead with our pre-arranged opening words.

The floor Manager gave us the countdown on his fingers 5 – 4 – 3 – 2 – 1 "We're live."

It was 11 pm at QVC The Shopping Channel's studio in Battersea and I was presenting the last of six shows that had begun with the launch of the telescope at midnight the previous evening.

The numbers weren't looking good for the T.S.V. (Todays Special Value) figures. The price was right £106, but we'd only sold 500 out of the 1,000 telescopes we had in stock and we were expected to sell at least 750.

In fairness, telescopes are some of the most difficult products to sell on TV because the viewer can't look down the lens. We can't point it at the sky. We can't show enlarged photos of the Moon, Mars and Saturn's rings, because that would misrepresent what people would actually see down the lens when they get it home.

During the break, Rob and I put our heads together to come up with an innovative way to boost the sales.

"I've got an idea" I told him. "During the last break I was chatting with the CEO of the telescope company and he told me a story that I think we can use."

Rob opened the show "Good evening and welcome to QVC The Shopping Channel. I am very excited to have with me here Dexter Moscow representing the prestige brand TASCO Telescopes who make precision optical instruments".

"Dex, tell me why should we buy this telescope"?

"Why buy this telescope Rob? Because the first time you look down the lens and experience the wonders of the galaxy you will be hooked for ever. Let me tell you a story that the M.D of TASCO told me. One cold November night he said to his seven-year-old daughter, 'Let's wrap up warm, take a flask of hot tomato soup and go into the garden, set up chairs and point the telescope at the moon'.

"He positioned the telescope and pointed it at the bright half-moon, the best time to view it. Set against the dark sky the craters of the moon stood out in sharp relief and they both gasped in awe.

"This experience created in his daughter a life-long love of astronomy and that moment together in the garden brought them closer together".

Guess how many telescopes were sold? By the end of the show, not a single telescope remained. We'd sold out. In that last hour we sold £53,000 worth of telescopes.

The lesson to learn here is that whether you are selling on TV, to your colleagues, the board, clients or customers story telling is the key to engagement, influence and persuasion.

My career path to becoming a QVC guest presenter, and for 16 years being their Chief Trainer on the Guest Excellence Programme drew on my experience in the advertising industry where my love of words was created. As an equity partner of a major North London estate agency practice I developed my passion for training others.

I taught negotiators how to sell and also the art of creating effective relationships with vendors, purchasers and colleagues.

After setting up my own estate offices and ultimately selling out to a major insurance company these skills came together when I was retained by Sainsbury's to purchase a street of houses and the forecourts of high street shops to enable them to build a superstore

This led to a recommendation from a friend who, hearing about my 'convincer strategies', asked me to sell a range of video recorders and other technology on QVC The Shopping Channel. I did not fully appreciate that QVC was in fact a TV channel that broadcasted live.

After a year of selling everything from technology for major brands to Christmas lights, trees and ornaments, in addition, I was asked to step behind the cameras and run a short course for their production assistants on how to effectively manage the expectations of guest presenters.

This led to me being sent to QVC's home office in the US to learn how they trained their guest presenters. I brought these ideas back to the UK, developed and adapted the programme to fit in with a more 'English style of selling.

On a visit to the UK the QVC's chief trainer in the US was so impressed with our training style she adopted elements of our Guest Excellence Course to run in America.

This experience and working with Reed International, The Dale Carnegie Organisation and The Sandler Sales Institute Training enabled me to develop the principles to be discussed in this book and to the overarching principle:

DON'T SELL - INFLUENCE OTHERS TO TAKE ACTION

Here are some more examples of how to sell a concept or an idea, rather than a product.

Could you 'sell' God to millions?

http://bit.do/DM-JL

The above link takes you to the video of a benediction given by Dr Joseph Lowery at the inauguration of Barack Obama.

I was amazed how on a wintry January day in 2009 two million Americans of many colours, creeds and backgrounds came together, braving the freezing

Washington air, to bear witness to this historic event. The inauguration of America's first black President, Barack Obama.

Dr Lowery, an elderly pastor, made his way slowly to the microphone and perfectly captured the mood and emotion of this most auspicious occasion.

It was not only the content of his presentation that captured my imagination, but also the style of his delivery. He started haltingly, but then his voice gained strength, as did the power and poetry of his words.

The following extract perfectly encapsulates the cleverness of his discourse:

"... we ask you to help us work for that day when black will not be asked to get in back, when brown can stick around ... when yellow will be mellow ... when the red man can get ahead, man; and when white will embrace what is right."

Two million people then, in a single joyous voice, joined with him to chant 'Amen, Amen, Amen'. How many of the countless millions watching throughout the world caught up in the moment joined with him chanting 'Amen'?

Also in the speech were many cleverly crafted biblical references "when tanks will be beaten into tractors" (swords into ploughshares) and noteworthy phrases that embraced people of other nations "when every man and every woman shall sit under his or her own vine and fig tree". In these few words he painted a picture of disadvantage, discrimination and repression that had been suffered for decades.

Using poetic devices Dr Lowery echoed the words of Barak Obama, encapsulated the emotions of the moment and restated the hope and promise of a less divided society.

What are the lessons you can learn from this speech to sell to your audience? How can you introduce arguments and proposition to influence others?

The answer:

You need to capture people's hearts before you can capture their minds.

This oration is an impressive demonstration of what creates power, impact and influence in verbal and non-verbal communication. Our perception of this elderly preacher changed as his voice became stronger, his body language became more commanding. The pace, tone of voice and his verbal tricks served to enthral us.

In any situation where you are seeking to move people to action you need to make an emotional connection.

Often in a corporate situation you need to change people's perception of you and the concepts illustrated above and those we will discuss in the following chapters will show you how.

A great presentation does not just happen. It follows a specific framework enabling you to prepare effectively, develop compelling content and deliver that content with power and impact. It has to have a dynamic, clear and specific message that engages your audience and compels them to take action.

I call that framework the M.O.S.C.O.W Method, a six-stage process that will enable you to conquer your public speaking fears and empower you to engage at the highest level.

Broadly it covers **four key areas** of presentation creation:

PREPARATION – STRUCTURE – CONTENT – DELIVERY

Preparation

The key to making an effective, engaging and enthralling presentation is to have the right attitude and mindset. Know how to still your nerves, so that the adrenalin works for you rather than incapacitates you.

It demands the gathering of essential information about the audience you are speaking to so that you get them onside before you even open your mouth. Research their level of seniority, interests and expertise and tailor your content, language and key messages to meet their expectations.

We will cover how to commit your thoughts to paper, review, edit and then revise your notes so that you don't have to read them and are able to maintain eye contact with your audience.

Structure

The touch points that take your audience from mere interest to 'Where do we sign?'

We'll identify:

- **The key elements that need to be included**
- **The hooks to hang the content on, so that when you sit down to write the presentation you know exactly how you are going to start**
- **What points you need to cover in the body of the talk**
- **How to finish with power and impact so that your audience knows exactly what you want them to do**

I will explore with you the frameworks that have enabled me to sell £ millions of products on QVC The Shopping Channel and to coach others to do the same. I will show how I use these to develop seminars, win business in the corporate arena and gain invitations as a keynote speaker at symposiums, exhibitions and major networking events.

Content

The specifics of what you are going to say lies at the core of your presentation.

Identify:

- The memorable phrases you need to construct
- The relevant stories you need to tell
- The style of language you need to adopt

This will ensure your audience is emotionally connected, so that all those present get the message and are prompted to take the action you desire them to take.

The crafting of the talk so that attention is maintained and recall is heightened. What actually does your audience want to know, as opposed to what you think they want to know? Assumption kills communication.

Often, the content of a presentation will fail because the message, business offering or concept does not take into account what the audience wants to hear, or their level of understanding of the subject you are talking about.

We get so caught up in the detail that we become too technical, too arrogant, or too condescending, expecting them to keep up. We use jargon or, worse still, initials and meaningless acronyms. We convey our own knowledge as if we are lecturing undergraduates rather than connecting with decision makers.

Delivery

This is all about the mechanics of how you are going to deliver your presentation.

What mechanisms will you use to convey the information you have so painstakingly prepared? PowerPoint (Lord help us), microphone (hand held, on a stand or lapel), flip charts (how many?), story boards, pictures, props, all need to be considered.

In today's world of instant gratification, if you have not captured your audience's interest in the first 30 seconds, you've lost them. You may know this if you have ever tried speed dating or done an 'elevator pitch' at a networking event.

Before you even open your mouth, judgments have been made about you that you will either change or confirm during the rest of your presentation.

Just look at the front row of folded arms to see if they have 'bought' into you. Some 85% of the message we deliver is initially perceived visually, then you have to ensure they stay with you. Your words, phrases and intonation become paramount. If they are still prepared to listen to you, should your tone of voice be monotonous or your delivery stilted, watch their eyes glaze over, their chins sink to their chest and their thoughts turn to the bar.

Your voice tonality and pace totally determines whether your message sinks in or sinks without a trace.

You need to create well-constructed phrases that enthral and delight and catch your audience's imagination. Otherwise you will have them hurriedly moving toward the exit door, grab for the TV remote to change channels, or leave your site with a click of the cursor or swipe of a finger.

Our senses are bombarded with information, 24 hour news, the internet, television, newspapers, billboards and our mobile phones. We are desensitised to reasoned argument, and crave easy-to-digest pieces of information.

Whether you are reporting to the Board, presenting to an audience of shareholders, fronting the yearly company-wide conference or making a speech at a friend's wedding, it is essential that you are totally conversant with a bewildering array of technologies. You need to be comfortable with projectors, PowerPoint, earpieces, lapel mics, and autocues.

When delivering your message via video, podcasts, audio files or the myriad of other technologies, to come across as less than assured, as hesitant or lacking in confidence, will weaken your argument. If you devalue your proposition you will miss an opportunity to impress.

Trust is the key. Lose this and you will fundamentally damage the reputation and financial stability of the organisation you represent.

Video, whether in its own right or as part of a longer presentation, is becoming an essential part of any performance. Accessed via YouTube, or directly from your website, it is an excellent means by which to promote your offering or convey important information. But it cannot be an 'in-your-face' sales pitch. It must be carefully thought through, engagingly presented and speak to what is happening in the world of your viewer.

Executives in today's corporate spotlight have to be more than good communicators; they have to be master influencers. That means that as part of your selling activities, you need to take centre stage.

Even if your heart is pounding, your hands are shaking and beads of sweat appear on your brow, you will have to take that long lonely walk to stand behind a slim polished aluminium column surmounted by a microphone. This is necessary in order to advance your career, grow your business or improve your profile.

At some point in your life you will have to literally step up to the mic.

The MOSCOW Method

The MOSCOW Method will enable you to conquer your public speaking fears and empower you to engage at the highest level. It will ensure that your presentation flows and is relevant to your audience. It is the culmination of over three decades of investigation, analysis and personal insight into the mysteries of personal persuasion and covers the six key areas to create a compelling presentation.

They are:

M – Mind Set

Before you influence and persuade others, be convinced yourself.

When asked to make a presentation, pitch or speech is your first reaction to duck the opportunity because you fear making a fool of yourself? Let's get the butterflies flying in formation

O – Objective

A good presentation entertains – A great presentation moves others to action.

It is not enough to know what we want to achieve out of the presentation, pitch, or proposal. If we do not have a mutual purpose we will only tell half the story.

S – Sensory Acuity

Keep your audience engaged, receptive and alert.

People perceive information in different ways. Sensory awareness enable you to know when you are losing them, how to control them and what to do to re-engage with them.

C – Congruency

What you say, how you say it and how you look when you say it must be in harmony.

Your body language, the clothes you wear, your voice tonality, the pace of your delivery and the phrases you use all have an impact on how you are perceived. This directly affects whether you are trusted and what you say is accepted.

O – Order

Take me on a journey of discovery and I will follow you.

A great presentation should be easy to follow. Each element should flow seamlessly together and take your audience on a journey that has a beginning, a middle and an end. What stories, anecdotes or jokes can you tell, what props can you use and what attention reset buttons do you need to press to get your message across?

W – Work the room

Prepare before, question during and verify after the presentation.

The key to a great talk that achieves each party's objective is to know, without a shadow of a doubt, what the audience want out of the interaction. Research before the event, question the audience before you take to the 'stage' and verify after.

•••••

As you make your way through each area of the MOSCOW method, you will learn easy-to-remember, easy-to-use processes to develop the essential areas of effective presentations, business-winning pitches and speech making that has the audience wanting more.

It is said that the journey of a 1,000 miles starts with a single step.

Your journey to making a compelling, enthralling and business winning presentation starts with a single purpose. To showcase your wealth of knowledge, illustrate your expertise and impart information to the benefit of you and your audience.

That specific information and content will follow. For now, let's get your head on straight, understand what you want to gain from your interaction and explore the mechanisms that will enable you to connect at a deep psychological level.

Why is it essential to connect at a deep psychological level? Because by understanding an individual's true motivation and tailor-making your pitch, presentation, proposition or conversation to those needs differentiates you from your competitors, colleagues and other suppliers.

It will enable you to be perceived differently.

Case Study

When I was a property consultant I was asked to negotiate the removal of a tenant with whom there had been a dispute over rent arrears, of a commercial building that needed to be redeveloped.

Solicitors had been instructed and a court date set. I was brought in to facilitate a more conciliatory approach.

Prior to meeting the tenant I made him fully aware that although I was acting on behalf of the Landlord I wanted to understand the situation from his point of view.

Sitting in his flat he showed me where promised repairs had not taken place and identified other areas where the landlord has been less than helpful.

We spoke for a couple of hours, to be exact he spoke for most of that time venting his anger, his frustration and his aspirations for the future.

Over the years I have found that this approach, giving people the opportunity to express their deep concerns, develops rapport and opens an opportunity to do the deal.

Ultimately, I walked the tenant out of the property to his bank and cashed a cheque that enabled him to realise his ambitions.

Allowing for court cost, solicitor's fees and the time saved in developing the site my client still came out on top.

Key Learning

The first step is to understand what is going on for them. Move away from what you want to convey to what they need to know. You need to shift your MIND SET.

Exercise 1 – Not what you do but why you do what you do.

Your first step is to identify why you are different in your market, your U.S.P. No, not your Unique Selling Point but your Unique Selling Proposition.

Not what you do, but *why* you do it. What is your purpose, your belief? What is it that motivates you to get up in the morning?

If you can't answer these questions ask your clients and customers. Why do they keep on using your services? Find this out and you may even get more work and perhaps referrals.

Need more information? Follow the link below:-

http://bit.do/DM-SS

> *Before you can convince others,*
> *you have to know who you are.*

Chapter 2

M – MINDSET

-----❖-----

Fear doesn't exist anywhere except in the mind.

Dale Carnegie American developer of self-improvement, salesmanship.

Billionaire investor Warren Buffett was terrified of public speaking. He was so nervous, in fact, that he would arrange and choose his college classes to avoid having to get up in front of people. He even enrolled in a public speaking course and dropped out before it even started.

"I lost my nerve," he said.

At the age of 21, He decided that to reach his full potential, he had to overcome his fear of public speaking. Buffett enrolled in a Dale Carnegie course with another thirty people who, like him, were "terrified of getting up and saying our names."

Once he was asked "What habits did you cultivate in your 20s and 30s that you see as the foundation of success?"

Buffett answered, "You've got to be able to communicate in life and it's enormously important. If you can't communicate and talk to other people and get across your ideas, you're giving up your potential."

Let's begin.

It has been said that people fear public speaking more than dying. The reality is that people fear public speaking because they don't want to die in front of an audience. Ask any performer. To forget their lines, not get that laugh, and leave the stage to the sound of one hand clapping or the hollow echo of their own footsteps is the worst experience in their life. They feel like they want to die.

It may not be that your life depends on your performance, but it certainly impacts on your lifestyle and livelihood.

If the thought of standing in front of an audience fills you with horror, or preparing for a business presentation feels like preparing for your own execution, it's not that you don't know your subject. It's the fear that you will present the knowledge that you do have in a way that leaves your audience totally unmoved or, at best, wondering what they need to do next.

If you are asked to say a few off-the-cuff words, does panic grip your stomach? Do you break out in a cold sweat? Do you suddenly need to rush to the loo, with the butterflies in your stomach feeling like they have just hatched into bats?

If this is you, I will show you some of the tricks that:

- Actors use to quell stage fright
- Seasoned keynote speakers use to prepare themselves mentally for their talks
- TV presenters use to calm themselves before the cameras start rolling.

In this chapter we will explore proven strategies to calm nerves, make your adrenalin work for you rather than against you and identify your successes to create stories that highlight your achievements and bolster your confidence.

We will graft this onto a methodology that prepares you for that important business or personal presentation.

When you are offered the opportunity of making a pitch or formal 'front of room' presentation what is your state of mind?

- Do you feel confident because you have done so many of them before?

- Or is your thinking clouded by how you feel and your first instinct is to pass the responsibility to someone else?

- Perhaps you fear that the impact you will make on your audience will damage your reputation

Is the voice in your head telling you: -

"I'm going to make a fool of myself"?

"They'll see that I am in a cold sweat"?

"I know that I am going red from ear to ear"?

"I need to rush to the loo and stay there".

In a corporate environment this can impact negatively on your chances of advancement, of impressing the board, or getting a project accepted. It may even lose you a sale.

At its extreme nerves can show up as a flying fear. One where the speaker literally runs from the impending presentation.

For most people however, nerves may express themselves in more subtle ways. When you are asked to make a presentation, do you duck the opportunity? This relinquishes your power and damages your prospects and rather than enabling you gives the chance to shine to someone else. At the minimum nerves just prevent you from being the best you can possibly be.

If this situation resonates with you here are some ideas to prevent you from missing out when the chance to stand out from the crowd comes to you.

Nerves are normal, in fact they are essential.

Every time I stand in front of an audience of one or many, present a product on TV, conduct a webinar, run a workshop or give a keynote speech I am nervous. The adrenaline rush nerves give you can enliven your presentation.

It gives it energy and leaves your audience with the **feeling** that you are passionate about your subject, proposition, concept and company.

I have highlighted the word feeling because the majority of things you say will be lost, but how you leave people feeling will stay with them.

Maya Angelou an American poet, writer, and civil rights activist, was famously quoted as saying: -

> *"People may forget what you said, they may forget what you did, but they will never forget how you made them feel".*

Let's however be realistic about the level of nerves. What level aids you and what level debilitates you?

Respond to this scenario honestly

You have been asked to make a presentation to the Board, have been given the opportunity to give a talk to your networking group or have been asked to speak at a friend's celebration.

On a scale of 1 – 10, where 1 is no nerves at all to 10 that is abject fear and horror, clear the way I'm out of here, what is your level of nerves?

- Are you between 7- 10? This means you are in a cold/hot sweat, you heart is beating so loud you can hear it, you feel the urge to run and your mind has gone blank.

- Is it around 4 – 6? Here your mouth goes dry, you stutter, hesitate, stumble or lose your words.

- If 2 – 3 you're in control, there is a flutter of nerve but that is good as you need that adrenaline kick. You will be confident and come across with authority.

- Your level is 1? No nerves at all? BEWARE! If you don't have the faintest feeling of nerves or are not experiencing a frisson of excitement then not only will your presentation be flat but you may come across as bored or even worse still condescending.

A great friend of mine, Julian Ballantyne, who for many years I worked with at QVC The Shopping Channel, both as a colleague on the Guest Excellence Workshops and opposite him as a guest presenter, had a pet phrase, *"Everybody suffers from butterflies, the trick is to get them to fly in formation"*.

Here are some ideas to enable you to get those butterflies to fly, not only in formation, but to perform some spectacular aerobatics.

Nerves provide me with energy... It's when I don't have them, when I feel at ease, that's when I get worried.

Mike Nichols Film Director

Getting the butterflies to fly in formation

The first process is **Visualisation**.

The techniques I use in my coaching have been developed by eminent doctors, psychologists and sports coaches, whose knowledge has been gained through scientific study, observation and experimentation

These are some practical examples of the success you can achieve by adopting these methodologies.

Imagine that

Have you ever fantasised that you're a lean, mean fighting machine, with Churchillian speech-making talents, winning charisma, and superhuman willpower? If so, then you have already tapped into the tool that can help you get there in real life.

Mental imagery—the kind that involves imagining success—has long been employed by professional athletes to boost their strength, confidence and results. But the technique is good for more than just sports.

"Everyone can use imagery to prepare for all kinds of situations, including public presentations and difficult interactions," says Daniel Kadish, Ph.D., an eminent psychologist in New York City who guides clients in mental imagery. Although Daniel works mainly with athletes, his approach is valuable to show you how to manage emotions and negative self-talk. It is worth learning more from his articles and studies.

Research has shown that surgeons, musicians and business executives have used it to focus and to improve their performance. It could also help you run a 5K, ace a presentation, or even pass up the morning doughnut box.

How it works

Scientists believe that we may experience real-world and imaginary actions in similar ways.

Aymeric Guillot, Ph.D., a professor at the Centre of Research and Innovation in Sport at University Claude Bernard Lyon, in France, has written about the connection between mental and motor imagery. He has examined the relationships between mental imagery and perception, and between motor imagery and physical execution.

Whether we walk on a mountain trail or only picture it, we activate many of the same neural networks—paths of interconnected nerve cells that link what your body does to the brain impulses that control it.

You can use this to your advantage in different ways. For example, imagining yourself doing movements can help you get better at them: Legendary golfer Jack Nicklaus practised each shot in his mind before taking it.

Mental workouts also stimulate the sympathetic nervous system, which governs our fight-or-flight response and causes increases in heart rate, breathing, and blood pressure.

So simply envisioning a movement elicits nervous-system responses comparable to those recorded during physical execution of the same action, says Guillot.

Although it may sound like hocus-pocus, some research suggests that imagining could help you get results even when you don't move a muscle.

In one notable study that appeared in the North American Journal of Psychology in 2007, athletes who mentally practised a hip-flexor exercise had strength gains. These gains were almost as significant as those in people who actually did the exercise (five times a week for 15 minutes) on a weight machine.

If your challenge is more mental than physical—for instance, handling a difficult conversation—imagery can keep you calm and focused.

"Mentally rehearsing maintaining a steady assertiveness while the other person is ignoring or distracting you can help you attain your goal," says Kadish.

Envisioning this calmness may also decrease physical symptoms of stress, like an increase in heart rate or stress hormones. When you repeatedly imagine performing a task, you may also condition your neural pathways so that the action feels familiar when you go to perform it; it's as if you're carving a groove in your nervous system.

In short mind over matter. Effective imagery can even enhance recovery of stroke patients so how much can it do more for us able bodied.

Finally, on a purely psychological level, envisioning success can enhance motivation and confidence.

The basics

Powerful though your mind may be, you can't just think your way from running a nine-minute mile to a five-minute one.

"Imagery can't make you perform beyond your capabilities, but it can help you reach your potential," says Tom Seabourne, Ph.D., an athlete and imagery expert and the author of The Complete Idiot's Guide to Quick Total Body Workouts (Amazon).

So imagery can be a handy tool the next time you have set your sights on a goal. Here's how to put it into effect.

Use all your senses. Mental imagery is often referred to as visualization, but it's not limited to the visual.

"The most effective imagery involves all five senses," says Michael Gervais, Ph.D., a performance psychologist in Los Angeles who has worked with numerous professional athletes and teams.

What are you smelling, hearing and feeling? "You should be so immersed in a mental image that it seems as if it is actually happening," he says.

Be the star, not the audience. To engage in your practice fully, "imagine performing the activity from your own perspective," says Seabourne. "Don't watch yourself as if you're viewing a movie."

Practice. "Effective mental imagery is not wishful thinking, nor is it brief moments of 'seeing' success," says Gervais. Just as you can't become a better speaker simply by reading a book on the subject, "the only way we get better at mental imagery is by practising it," says Tammy Miller, a speech coach in State College, Pennsylvania.

Write it down. If you really want to hone your efforts, put the story of how your feat will unfold in writing, says Kay Porter, Ph.D., a sports-psychology consultant and the author of The Mental Athlete (Amazon).

Get specific

You can further enhance your practice if you employ strategies specific to your goal. Use these tips to meet challenges that are especially – well – challenging.

If you want to ace the speech...

Gervais recommends that you script your success. Break up the imagery into segments.

- First imagine walking into the room. What is the lighting like? The temperature? What are you wearing?

- Then take a deep breath before you begin.

- Think of getting onstage with the sense of trusting yourself, says Porter.

- Look into the audience and focus on one or two people who are interested in what you're saying as you deliver the speech calmly and smoothly. But don't picture everything going perfectly.

- Also rehearse overcoming difficulty," says Kadish. "You might envision someone yawning loudly, but experience yourself maintaining your focus and delivery."

- Be true to yourself. If you're a soft-spoken type, don't visualise yourself thundering and pounding your fists; it won't feel real. Think of speaking clearly and confidently, as the very best version of you.

Client Case Study - International Franchise Event

My client is a major high street retailer. Twice a year the buying team has to present the upcoming ranges of clothes, toys and accessories to a room of forty to fifty worldwide franchise partners.

The team had always experienced a high level of anxiety and tension at these events, because the franchise partners constantly interrupt the presentations and make adversarial and dismissive comments. They look at their phones, have conversations amongst themselves and are up and down in their seats and roaming around the room.

The buyers, merchandisers and designers established way of showing the new seasons ranges was to read a brief description from a card. They would then go through the products one by one identifying them by item number, price and with only a minimal amount of information given about the design rationale.

This delivery was very flat, monotonous and, obviously, the franchisees just switched off, preferring to read the notes in their folders.

After four days of this style of presentation the franchise partners, unsurprisingly, were bored. In most cases they were confused about what ranges they should buy and probably forgot most of what they had been told.

Knowing that these events were pretty much a disaster and the year-on-year sales were down 10%, my brief was to build the team's confidence, enthusiasm and skills to manage the room and deal with the negative feedback that they often received.

I reviewed everything from the room layout to product information, from content to delivery. In essence, my brief was to create an event that would energise, motivate, enthral and influence and persuade the franchise partners to buy more.

I changed the room layout from theatre style to cabaret style making it a more intimate setting in which the team could consult and present. On each table we placed a member of the international team, buyers and merchandisers to field questions and develop closer relationships with the franchisees.

The team used presentation frameworks and processes that we will discuss in later chapters. This allowed their personalities to shine through, giving them the authority to explain the design concept, why they were personally excited by what they had created and the reasons why they had used various cartoon and other characters in the product ranges.

Using guided visualisation, I helped them to envisage themselves being applauded, congratulated and thanked for developing the ranges. They imagined the franchise partners smiling, nodding in agreement and a line of people waiting to meet and do business with them.

This new-style event created an entirely different atmosphere in the room, the result of which was a 12% increase in sales from what had been a 10 % deficit. The team received plaudits from the franchise partners for the new seasons range and for creating the best four-day sales conference ever.

Treatment for a PHOBIC response

For some people the feeling in the stomach is not butterflies, but writhing snakes of terror that make them want to run. At its extreme this a phobic response and is based on an experience that is so profound that it colours a person's attitude to life.

Phobias are often formed in an instant. A fear of spiders may have been created by one dropping on your hand as a child. A fear of heights may have been developed from falling off a slide in the playground.

These programmed responses are then imbedded into your psyche and come to the surface in adulthood. When you see a scurrying spider, stand at the top of a steep escalator or on a precipice all these subdued fears rush back.

The following is a visualisation process that has been developed out of the research of Richard Bandler, the inventor of NLP – Neuro Linguistic Programming. This process acknowledges that people perceive information in different ways. Most of us have a natural tendency to take information in via either visual (seen), auditory (heard) or kinaesthetic (touch) stimuli.

There's more detail about this in later chapters, but at this point you should be aware of these elements when constructing your presentation.

This methodology has its roots in the work of Milton H Erickson, an American psychiatrist and psychologist specialising in medical hypnosis and family therapy.

A basic phobia treatment procedure

Imagine that you are in a large empty cinema with the screen in front of you.

Think of a time when you experienced the phobic response. It does not have to be the first time, but it is more powerful if you can remember that. On the screen view the experience as a movie with you in the audience watching it.

Then float yourself back out of the audience in order to see yourself in the audience. Look at yourself sitting there watching the movie you're 'starring' in.

Then imagine yourself in the projection booth watching yourself in the audience watching the movie on the screen. This creates what is known as a double dissociation.

You are not watching the screen directly, but you are watching yourself watching the person watching the screen.

Firstly, you watch the movie forwards. Then watch the movie backwards.

You can then change the action in playful ways such as using cartoon characters with squeaky voices.

When the movie is finished, float back from the projection booth into the audience.

Then float from the audience onto the screen into yourself at the end of the movie and run it backwards multiple times very fast.

You can do this more than once, until you feel your emotions are in check.

A real life case study - My fear of spiders

This dated back to the time when my brother put a spider in my bed and when I pulled back the sheet it ran down the covers and disappeared into the fold of the blankets. I then recalled completely stripping the covers, shaking them thoroughly and remaking my bed.

By using the visualisation process described above I was able to have a tarantula crawl from one hand to the other without any sense of fear or repulsion.

Before We Can Influence Others, We Have to Influence Ourselves

There is an often used acronym defining F.E.A.R as a False Expectation Appearing Real.

It indicates that a large percentage of our negative self-talk around what we fear never actually occurs.

This concept has now been proved in a study conducted by researchers at the University of Cincinnati. They found that 'eight-five percent (yes – 85%) of what we worry about never happens. Moreover, the study found that 79% of us handle the 15% that does happen in ways that surprise us with our ability to turn the situation around'.

I like to think of that feeling as Feeling Excited Anticipating Rewards. In fact, if you think of the physical manifestation of fear – shallow breathing, clammy hands and butterflies in the tummy – it bears an uncanny resemblance to the physical symptoms of excitement. Strangely, in the early stages of a relationship we exhibit the same symptoms when the object of our affection appears!

Armed with this knowledge, in addition to the visualisation techniques discussed above, you can start to re-programme your brain to work for you rather than against you.

Take time to recall your personal success stories and write them down. They don't have to be earth shattering, they have to be meaningful to you.

The Power of Story Telling

This three-element process will enable you to construct compelling, concise and relevant stories that not only empower you, but allow your audience to step into your experience and share it with you. Your stories should paint a vivid picture that shares a real-life experience. It should be emotionally engaging, sensory rich and an experience that offers a clear and specific beneficial lesson or key message that you want to convey at the end.

Some may call these stories parables of life, a snapshot of your history or a journey that you are inviting your listener to take with you.

To be truly impactful a story, like a joke, should be short, it should have resonance in the audience's world and leave them with a sense that they have experienced it along with you.

Positive experience exercise

In my seminars I ask the delegates to think of a story that is a positive experience or illustrates a life lesson that they want to impart to others. One that, when they think about it, really excites them.

You are looking for a story that you feel was a major achievement that made you feel proud, energised, or had a profound positive effect on your life. It can be taken from any moment in your life.

It should be no more than two minutes long and divided and timed into these three sections.

Incident

This should set the scene for the story and describe the overarching incident/issue/problem. **(30 seconds).**

Action

This illustrates what actually happened. How did you resolve the issue?

The words you use should tap into all our senses. The sounds, the colours, the feelings, the smells. Everything that brings the story alive in your listeners' minds. **(75 seconds)**

Benefit /Outcome

What was the benefit, life lesson, consequence to you as the storyteller, the company, the team, the individual?

To enhance the benefit statement further it should be encapsulated in 5 -7 words. Like a tag line or newspaper headline. **(15 seconds)** The beneficial effect of this exercise is that it enables you to think of your successes rather than focus on your failures. It allows you to create a store of relevant and engaging anecdotes that you can sprinkle throughout your presentation.

It shows the human side of you and can be worn like a cloak of confidence when you are faced with daunting situations.

It allows you to say to yourself, 'if I did this at that time, I can do this now'.

Whenever my wife is faced with a situation that she feels she cannot overcome, she remembers the time that she accomplished the Fire Walk at an Anthony Robbins seminar. She says to herself "If I was able to walk across hot coals, I can do this". It's her benchmark for facing a seemingly impossible task.

As with the start to a presentation a story should also have an opening that makes an impact and gets the audience's attention.

Exercise 2 – Your Success Stories

What are the success stories, the case studies, the problems you have resolved for others that you can illustrate in a story format?

Make it relevant to the audience you are speaking to and make it as descriptive as possible, so they feel that they are stepping into the experience with you.

Remember, it's not about what you do, but what you have done for others.

Illustrate the problem and the positive outcomes achieved. Quantify the result if you can.

Chapter 3

O – OBJECTIVE

-----❖----

Assumption kills communication and the 'deal'

A couple with their two children came into my estate agency office one Saturday at 5:30 pm and wearily sat down.

Instead of asking for their name, address and requirements, as most agents would, I said "You look like you have had a very long and tiring day. Can I get you and the kids something to drink"?

I handed to the children magazines and comics that I kept for these situations. It would keep them occupied, while I asked their parents how I could help them.

Once the family had had a few sips of their drinks and chomped on some biscuits I asked, "So what have you seen today that you liked or didn't like"?

By establishing immediate rapport, I did something they weren't expecting and made them feel comfortable. I asked an open question that would help me understand what they were really looking for, and why.

I knew that a family who had spent all day Saturday looking for property and, at the end of that day, were still looking, were in the market to buy and that the search was time-sensitive or urgent.

It was only when I'd put them at ease that I asked them about their situation, where they had travelled from, had they a property to sell, and many other questions to establish where they were in their search for property.

Then I repeated back to them their requirements in exactly the language they had used to me.

This is a good method to gain people's trust so that they then perceive you differently. Rather than a sales person or one with an ulterior motive they see you as an individual who is sincerely interested in them.

I spent the early evening with them viewing suitable properties and building a close rapport.

Although on that Saturday we did not find the right property to close a deal, on the following Wednesday, I received instructions on a property that I thought would be ideal and phoned them. They told me that they had received this property from another agent and were just about to phone me to see if I had it.

We viewed the property together; they made an offer, which was accepted, and the sale went through.

Now that you have changed your mindset to ensure that you are feeling empowered, what else is going through your mind?

"How can I make sure I don't sound boring?"

"Will the audience get the message?"

"What is my message?"

"What is there that I can sell to the audience?"

"Will I impress them and advance my career?"

"Should I reach for the PowerPoint deck that I always use?"

ME - ME - ME

Wrong

The reality is that if you are focused on **you** and what **you** can get out of the interaction your basic premise is wrong.

When all you are worried about is how you are going to perform, your nerves kick in; you are full of self-doubt and anxiety.

However, when the focus is on the audience and you think: -

"What is going to be most relevant to them?"

"What are the reasons they are attending or have invited me to speak to them?"

"What would be the take-home from the talk, pitch or presentation that will add value to their lives, organisations or businesses?"

"Who are the audience, one or many?"

"What are the business problems they are experiencing that I may be able to resolve for them?"

"What are their personal fears, worries, challenges that are keeping them awake at night?"

THEM - THEM – THEM

Right

You know what you want. You want to get your message across so that you win a contract, gain the support of your colleagues, achieve advancement or convince others to at least meet with you.

Your starting point however, must always be to ask: What does the audience want? What is it that is causing your prospects, colleagues, clients or customers aggravation, anxiety, fear, worry and PAIN? What keeps them awake at night, causing problems in their home life, preventing them from moving forward in their careers, holding back their businesses? This myriad of tensions and frustrations **is your responsibility to find out**.

Notice that this agenda is all very personal. It's not just about their business situation. Be aware, though, that you need to ask permission to gain answers to these questions.

It is said that no deal was ever done without a conversation, and you need to talk to your existing clients in various sectors to discover the answers to the questions identified above, and how your interventions have resolved those issues.

When invited to speak at a conference, conduct a seminar, make a business pitch or a corporate presentation it is your duty to find out what's going on for your audience. So where do you go to gain the insight that will turn your presentation into business-winning opportunities that address the issues, both business and personal, that your attendees are facing?

If it is a conference, seminar, symposium or networking event, ask the organisers for a delegate list. Find out what the key issues are for them and which are the ones they feel are concentrating their minds. Find out what are the problems in that sector.

Don't use the word 'challenges'. Use the word 'problems'. Why am I being so pedantic about these words?

Because semantics are very important. Understanding the impact of words is essential. For me challenges are issues that can be overcome. We throw down the imaginary gauntlet and pick up the challenge. 'Problems' however are perceived as situations that cannot be overcome without help, advice and the views of others.

If it is a company event or an inter-departmental presentation where you are seeking to gain the support of your team, seniors and colleagues, speak to those individuals whose opinion you trust. Then develop your talk around those issues.

Where major organisations or companies are attending, use the internet to discover what is being said about them on Twitter, Facebook and LinkedIn. What are the CEO, MD, and CFO saying about the company on their website?

Armed with this kind of information, you can make your presentation relevant, your information rich, and you can gain buy-in for your proposals.

When you do this, you become genuinely interested in other people, (as Carnegie expressed it in his Principle number 4).

Life Lesson 1 – Focusing on Them

One of the first life lessons I learnt from my time as an estate agent was that, when you focus on other people's needs and seek to find out about them, then an immediate connection is made.

The reality is people hate being sold to, they love being understood and consulted.

You need to develop rapport at a very early stage of your interaction. You need to use their language and not paraphrase what they have said. You need to tune into their emotional state.

This is exactly what happened in the story at the beginning of this chapter.

Key Learning

When you take the time to make an **EMOTIONAL CONNECTION** you can influence and persuade rather than have to 'sell'.

Life Lesson 2 – Walk in Their Shoes

Because of the effort I put into understanding the family's needs and related to them as human beings rather than focusing on the deal, I developed an emotional connection and a relationship based on TRUST.

Dale Carnegie in his book *How to win friends and influence people* identified 30 human relationships principles. Number 17 states "Try honestly to see things from the other person's point of view".

When you focus your MINDSET on this principle you reduce your anxiety and become an even more powerful influencer.

You need to find a way to develop that TRUST so that people believe what you say you can do and you can demonstrate that you will actually do it.

Whether it be one-to-one or one-to-many, creating that understanding of need is essential and informs what you present. It moves you out of your own head and into theirs.

In this way you can shape the content of your presentation by understanding the context in which it should sit. You can present ideas and concepts that are readily accepted because you have developed a deep understanding of your audience's needs.

When you ask yourself, what is the pain the people you are seeking to influence are suffering and your response begins "I think ..." or "I assume ...", you are already on a losing pathway. If you don't know, you must find out.

Key Learning

When you do this, you create an essential element that will deliver greater business opportunities and consensus from your seniors, teams and colleagues – **TRUST.**

Today, trust in all aspects of our society is at an all-time low. In every part of our life we have been sold a lie. We have been let down by our Bankers, our Politicians, our Churches, the Police, the leaders of industry, commerce and the Utility companies. Every day in our newspapers there is a new revelation of how we have been misled by those in positions of authority and power.

Now we understand the value of gaining a clear insight into the emotional state of our audiences and the daily problems and fears they face. But how do you speak to those fears, differentiate yourselves from the crowd and turn an interesting talk into one where they take the action you want them to take?

We hate being sold to. People do not attend an event to hear an extended sales pitch. They have come to find a solution to their problems, a nugget of information and insight that will make their lives better. Your main objective is to offer them a solution to their immediate difficulty while opening their eyes to the fact that there are other issues that need to be tackled and you are the only person that can resolve those issues.

Your objective in your presentation is to peel back the layers of onion skin around their dilemmas and show that the problem they have brought to the session is not the real problem. Their problem lies three or four levels underneath.

David Sandler of the Sandler Sales Institute says: "Our job is to scratch away at the surface of the problem to make it feel uncomfortable, then we carry on rubbing until it becomes a sore, then dig deeper so that it becomes a wound and leave our prospects with the feeling that we are the only person who really understands their difficulties and can resolve their dilemma."

When you go to the doctor with, say, an ache in your arm, you would feel very ill used if all you were given was a paracetamol and asked to report back in a week. Of course this doesn't happen. What actually happens is the doctor will ask us questions to determine what has been going on.

What exercise have you been undertaking?

Have you been lifting any heavy objects?

Where does it hurt?

When does it hurt, and how long has it been hurting?

He or she will ask many questions to ascertain the root cause of the ache, not just identify the symptom.

So it should be with you, in your address. You should view yourselves as a doctor trying to find the real reason behind the surface discontent. Don't just seek the symptom, find the root cause. If you do any less you should be sued for malpractice!

There are four questions that I ask the delegates to answer prior to any workshop or talk I am asked to give on presentation and pitching.

> To ensure this workshop is relevant to your needs, in confidence, please send me your answers to the following questions:
>
> - Who are you presenting/pitching/speaking to, and seeking to influence and persuade?
>
> - How are you presenting/pitching/speaking to them?
>
> - How effective are your presentations/pitches/conversations?
>
> - What would be most helpful to gain from the proposed sessions?"

I collate the replies and, armed with this information, I create a relevant, informed and captivating presentation.

It doesn't matter if you receive very few or no responses, they don't know that, and you can still pepper your talk with situations that you know are relevant to them. What you have demonstrated by giving them the opportunity to respond is that they understand that the talk is focused on their needs.

If this information is not available in advance – whatever the reason - arrive at the event early, circulate and introduce yourself to the attendees as the speaker for the evening/day. Ask them the questions above and remember what is said to you about their problem, including their names (always ask permission to use the information and their names in your presentation).

The key here is flexibility, because what you find out may change what you need to say.

When you use real situations and people's names it closes the gap between you as a presenter and them as the audience, and shows that you are sincerely interested in removing their pain.

Your objective, once you have finished your presentation, is to elicit questions from the floor and gain a line of individuals wanting to speak to you.

If you do not have their contact details, ask for them, confirming that you will send them follow-up notes, a white paper or some extra information that will benefit them. Make it clear that, once they've left the talk, you will give them a follow-up call to explore how you might help them further. Do this within 48 hours of the presentation.

Let me give you an example of how a well-researched, relevant and information-rich presentation resulted in follow-up calls from instructing solicitors and legal briefs being awarded to a technically brilliant barrister.

Client Case Study - A Barrister's Journey

Profile

As a barrister, this person is accomplished at arguing cases in court. Most of his cases are white collar crimes, fraud, contract disputes and irregular financial dealings. He is always well prepared and knows the relevant case studies to research and quote from, and is able to prepare a reasoned argument.

He is able to persuade the Judge and, where necessary, a jury, impressing them with a convincing overview of the facts of the case. He is able not only to disseminate facts, but also to make complex points of law intelligible, and clarify areas that may otherwise have led to misunderstandings.

He is accomplished at challenging the opposing attorney's points of law, thinking on his feet and calling upon his knowledge and research of the case.

Problem

However, in situations where he needed to address a group of people to promote himself, and speak without a fully prepared script, he would become very nervous, hesitant and unsure. He was uncomfortable at the prospect of having to 'sell' himself, especially to an audience of people he did not know. To "brag about", his words, how great he was in court. There was also a lack of confidence, and a perceived inability to connect with the audience. He was told that his delivery was wooden, lacked spontaneity and was over-rehearsed, as indeed it was.

The compelling reason for him to improve was to gain more business. It was essential that he came across as confident, authoritative and knowledgeable and was able to hold his ground in front of instructing solicitors, clients and at networking meetings.

The specific situations in which he wanted to be more effective were to present at seminars, at networking meetings, at breakfast meetings and in larger gatherings, where it is of value to connect with people whom he did not know.

Solution 1 – What Does the Audience Want To Know?

The first priority was to identify what the audience of instructing solicitors wanted to know. This meant deciding upon a compelling topic that they would see as relevant, one where they were experiencing confusion or difficulty and one where they would gain an immediate benefit from hearing an informed speech.

The barrister's objective was to impress the audience with his knowledge and be seen as the only person who could resolve the solicitor's dilemmas and win cases. In this instance the compelling topic was the confusing area of law dealing with expert witnesses and how far they could be coached and persuaded to change their findings to suit the specific case. This is a very grey area of the law that solicitors find very challenging.

By identifying relevant case studies, illustrating how they had been effectively used in a specific case and the successful result, the barrister showcased his ability to disseminate and use complex information.

This offered an insight into the process he used and what had been achieved for his clients and, by implication, illustrated what could be achieved for the instructing solicitor's clients.

Solution 2 – Building Confidence

In court the barrister is confident, robust, well prepared and successful. However, in presentation situations his confidence evaporated. We explored how the skills shown in the courtroom could be translated to his presentation situations.

The Process

We worked with proven presentation frameworks where the barrister's expertise and knowledge could be showcased to gain business.

We used visualisation techniques that enabled him to control his nerves and focus on a positive outcome. To visualise himself in his wig and gown and act as if he were in the courtroom. This enabled him to feel empowered and confident.

Using these 'mind tricks' he became more influential and persuasive at the front of the room, and delivered his key messages with power and impact.

By understanding personality types and the way in which people receive and perceive information he was able to **Engage**, **Enlighten**, **Excite** and **Entertain** his audience. This gained buy-in and generated business opportunities.

These **E's** are the four strategic pillars of every powerful presentation, pitch or keynote speech.

The understanding of personality types and how people perceive information is an essential element of *Engagement* and cover the following areas. In terms of **D.I.S.C personality profiling** people are predominately:

- **Dominant –** A person who places emphasis on accomplishing results, the bottom line, confidence.

- **Influencers –** A person who places emphasis on influencing or persuading others, openness, relationships.

- **Steadiness –** A person who places emphasis on cooperation, sincerity, dependability.

- **Conscientiousness –** A person who places emphasis on quality and accuracy, expertise, competency. They need to receive information in specific ways and are predominately:

  - **Visual** - They need to see the information

  - **Auditory** - Words are important and they fneed to understand what is being said

  - **Kinaesthetic** – They need to *feel* that they can trust you and want to process the information

The Result

In the words of the Barrister:

"After many, many, more iterations of my talk and slides, and an inordinate amount of practice, I presented the experts topic to a commercial firm of solicitors. The feedback I got was that it was at the 'top of the premier league' of talks they had heard. They were positive that significant work would arise from this event".

The ultimate result of the presentation was that the barrister gained a number of lucrative briefs and a reputation for clear thinking based on carefully researched case studies.

Key Learning

The key learning for him was that personalising the examples (case studies) and their experience in using them worked particularly well.

There is a saying: **"No one ever got fired for hiring Microsoft"**.

Which means that reputation, illustration and TRUST are the keys to unlocking a customer's/client's concerns about your ability to do what you say you can do. The golden rule is: -

Don't tell people what you do – tell them what you have done for others.

In this way the listeners can paint themselves into your picture, identify situations that they have found themselves in and understand that only you can help them. They understand that you fully appreciate what they are going through, both personally and from a business perspective.

The case for trust...

How it is the Key to Winning an Argument

Every day in our newspapers there is a new revelation of how we have been misled by those in positions of authority and power.

How did the Conservative Party, led by Prime Minister Theresa May, lose the 12-point advantage they had over Labour prior to her calling a snap General Election in June 2017? What were the key elements that ultimately meant they suffered an ignominious humiliation at an election they were expected to win comfortably?

This is not an analysis from a political standpoint, but an outsider's view of how personality, language, the use of social media, an individual's authenticity and TRUST played a key role in persuading and influencing an unexpectedly large proportion of the voting public to get behind Jeremy Corbyn and give Theresa May a bloody nose?

Personal Impact And The Pound in Our Pocket - Not Policy

The issue of trust is demonstrated well by our response to the people who lead our country. Have you noticed how the political landscape has changed over the last number of elections? Policy has become less important. It is the way in which Members of Parliament and PMs understand us and appeal to us personally that are the foremost reasons and motivations as to why we are prepared to back them and give them our trust.

Thatcher vs Callaghan. Margaret Thatcher was perceived as a strong leader who would reduce the power of the unions. On the other side of the political divide was Jim Callaghan. He was not elected Prime Minister but succeeded Harold Wilson. Then, to his detriment, he presided over the 'Winter of Discontent'; a period of severe industrial disputes and strikes in 1978/79. This had a personal impact on the voters. Callaghan appeared weak, Thatcher appeared as our champion.

Major vs Kinnock. John Major, although the 'grey man' of politics, seemed to appeal to the electorate through his personal style of standing on an upturned soap box amid the crowds and getting out to meet them en masse.

Neil Kinnock, on the other hand, ran a much slicker campaign, but made a tactical error when, on taking to the stage at the Sheffield arena to a mighty ovation, was seen to punch the air chanting three times "We're all right." "We're all right." "We're all right."

It was reminiscent of a Nazi salute and the words 'Seig Hail'. Kinnock believes that this 'rush of blood to the head' cost him victory in the 1992 election. I believe also that his self-congratulatory stance was his undoing whereas Major was seen as one of the people.

Major vs Blair.   Although John Major, by many, is considered the best Conservative Prime Minister of modern times, he lost out to the considerably more charismatic Tony Blair. With his statesman-like persona, his seemingly centralist stance and realignment of the party to 'New Labour', Blair was like a Labour Thatcher and appealed not only to Labour supporters, but also to many Conservative voters.

Personal impact – not policy.

Brown vs Cameron.   Noting that Gordon Brown was, like Callaghan, not an elected leader, but rather an heir presumptive when Blair left office, this dour, unsmiling Scotsman was not the type of man the electorate took to their hearts.

Brown's premiership also coincided with the global recession and the near collapse of the banking system. Trust was damaged beyond repair. David Cameron on the other hand was young, vibrant and an excellent orator. A seeming saviour of both our finances and the countries.

Brown may have been policy strong but it was cameron's personality that appealed

So now we come to **May vs Corbyn.**   Again, in the case of Theresa May, she was a leader who was not elected by the country, but by her own party. She took over when Cameron, weakened by the Brexit vote, resigned. She came across as a Thatcher clone. Strong, stable and appearing to be someone we could trust to battle against the tribes of Europe.

In the campaign she came across as strong, yes, but lacking the common touch. She was great at Prime Minister's Question Time in the Commons, but poor when quizzed by the public.

Her campaign concentrated on the Brexit negotiations, but forgot about the people and was misled by her advisors who pressed forward with misguided and unpalatable policies.

She came across as robotic, uncaring, evasive, without empathy and most damaging of all, U-turned on budgetary strategy.

Jeremy Corbyn on the other hand came across as principled and targeted the personal fears of the electorate. The concerns of the young in schools, the burdens of university students' fees and the problem of financing the care of the elderly in their own homes.

Each negative message was carefully crafted and fed to the public via social media. Corbyn's image was transformed from a look-alike, shambolic, Michael Foot to a smart, suited and booted PM in waiting. He got down and dirty with the public holding presidential style gatherings surrounded by his loyal supporters.

He took part in debates and TV interviews and came across as a 'man of the people'. His personal ratings rose as May's fell.

Even faced with negative analysis of his manifesto spending plans by The Institute of Fiscal Studies, the financially inept interviews of both himself and Dianne Abbott, a large proportion of the voting public still supported him.

With the aftermath of the terrorist attacks in May and June, Corbyn was always there offering comfort and solace to the bereft public. Electioneering perhaps but, in contrast, May stayed away. At each turn she got it wrong and he got it right. She concentrated on policy; he was focused on the people.

He reiterated their fears using their words. He spoke to them via Twitter, Facebook and other online social media channels. His speeches were strong and delivered with passion.

His message was constant and unwavering. 'Labour is for the many, not the few'. This slogan was emotionally charged, concise and struck at the very root of how the Tories are perceived – elitist.

With all this stacked against Mrs May, she missed a golden opportunity. An opportunity to redress the emotional balance and come across as caring and empathetic.

Having refused to attend a public televised debate of all the major parties, at the last minute, Mr Corbyn decided he would attend. He had wrong-footed May again and, if she had suddenly declared that she would after all attend, this would have weakened her further.

But, she had been given a golden 'get out of jail card'

Amber Rudd, who was due to attend the debate in Mrs May's place, had just lost her father. What May should have done was to say:

"As Amber's father has sadly passed away it would be unfeeling and unfair of me to allow her to face the barrage of questions in her grief stricken state. Therefore, I will attend in her place so she can be with her family."

In one stroke she would have appeared caring, protective, authentic and a true leader. One that we could TRUST to care for us. But she didn't and the rest is, as they say, history.

The way in which the Conservative campaign was conducted addressed the logic of the situation and omitted the key element by which people make 'buying decisions' **EMOTION**. Remember, **'people buy emotionally, they decide logically'**.

Exercise 3 – what is your expertise?

What is it that you do that demonstrates your specific expertise?

What is a skill born out of your experience that others will find insightful?

As the Barrister did, create your own case studies.

Chapter 4

S – SENSORY ACUITY

-----❖----

Heightened awareness leads to heightened success

Let us not look back in anger, nor forward in fear, but around in awareness.

James Thurber

"Mr Moscow, you are unprofessional." Mr Khan announced in a raised angry voice, down the phone.

The hackles on the back of my neck stood up. I pride myself on my professionalism and this was a slight I was not prepared to take.

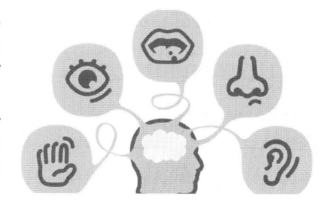

I responded aggressively, *"What do you mean unprofessional? I did exactly as you wanted me to. I delivered a pile of estate agents details so that you could research what was available on the market in your area."*

"That may be so Mr Moscow, but when I went round to see the agents they did not know anything about me." Mr Khan was still irate.

With the same level of irritation in my voice I said "Mr Khan that was not the deal. All I said I would do was to research the property in your vicinity and leave the details on your door step. In fact, you would not even let me in your house. You made it very clear that you were never going to move".

Adding, still irritated, "All I have ever wanted to do was come and see you."

After a short silence Mr Khan said "I'm available on Tuesday."

"That's not convenient," I said, "I'll be with you Thursday at 6:30 in the evening.

Mr Khan's house was one of the last houses in a street of houses that I had purchased on behalf of Sainsbury's for a new store in Kenton. We needed to use part of the rear garden to improve the footprint of the store.

Thursday arrived and I sat outside Mr Khan's house wondering how I could persuade this man to sell his house. Even at the inflated market price Sainsbury's were prepared to pay he was still not interested in moving.

A thought then suddenly came to me; histories.

I stepped up to the front door and rang the bell. Mr Khan opened the door and with a belligerent look on his face looked me up and down. I was ushered into the front room.

"Mr Khan before we sit down, tell me your history."

He proceeded to tell me that he had lived in Iraq and when there had been a change of government the situation for him, as a professor, had become untenable and he had to leave. He moved to Iran.

Further upheaval ensued when the Shah of Iran was deposed and Mr Khan had to move on again. That's when he came to England.

I stopped him there. "Mr Khan, I apologise. You have been dispossessed twice in your life and I am seeking to do it a third time. We will find a way to build the store without disturbing you."

His demeanour changed immediately. He brought out a bottle of whisky, placed it in front of us and we drank half a bottle together (although I don't drink spirits).

Ultimately we did the deal and he got one of the highest pay outs in the street. He even asked me to carry out a survey on the house he was buying, although I am not a surveyor. He trusted me enough to want my input.

*The life lesson I learnt very early on was, if you want to do business with somebody, **first understand their history.***

What is Sensory Acuity?

It is a phrase used in Neuro Linguistic Programming. It is an approach to communication that deals with the ability to be more aware of everything that is going on around you. The benefit of increasing your sensory acuity is a capacity to read the mood of your audience.

Why is that important to you?

Because it heightens your awareness if you are losing their attention and enables you to do something about it.

It will give you an ability to read people and understand how they need to receive and perceive information so that they more readily accept your proposition.

It will:

- Enable you to engage, or re-engage, and retain their attention
- Offer insights in how to deliver information effectively to a diverse audience
- Help you to know when to use PowerPoint or to consider alternatives.

Sensory Acuity is an essential skill for anyone involved in developing business connections, winning higher level contracts and influencing and persuading your colleagues, customers and audiences. It is an awareness of the mood of the people around you and the audience in front of you. That sensitivity allows you to keep them engaged.

It is the capacity, through our sense of sound, vision and feelings, to read the attitude of others and, if necessary, to adapt your presentation to engage with them at a deep psychological level.

For me Bill Clinton is the epitome of sensory acuity and awareness.

At a Downing Street function where he was the guest of honour, although surrounded by dignitaries, when he spoke to you it was as if there was nobody else in the room. His eye contact made you feel important, listened to and he was fully engaged in the conversation.

An example of his ability to use language and connect at a psychological level is illustrated by a situation that occurred during his Presidential Election campaign. He was running desperately short of funds and there was a very real chance that he would not be able to continue his race to the White House.

Having very close friends and supporters in the movie business he arranged to meet with a prominent film producer and close friend. He explained that if he was not able to raise $80,000 dollars it would be over. He said that this would be his 'High Noon', referring to an American multi-Oscar-winning film of the 1950s

The plot of the film centres on a town marshal who must face a gang of killers alone and has been subjected to various ideological interpretations. Some critics see the film as a symbolic allegory about American foreign policy. Marshal Kane wants to maintain peace as did Clinton with his Middle East peace process.

This clever use of imagery, tapped into the movie mogul's sensibilities and view of the world. Suffice it to say Clinton got the money he needed.

This awareness of how people perceive information is critical to enable you to be similarly persuasive.

People perceive information in different ways, as we identified in the last chapter. They could be:

- **Visual people**, who are more prepared to accept information that is delivered via pictures and images, by reading written material and hearing words that are highly descriptive. They speak quickly and, to tap into their mode of understanding, you need to draw pictures with your words so that they can step into the experience and see themselves in the situation. "Picture this", "See what I mean", "Let me draw your attention to".

- **Auditory people** who are more prepared to accept information that is delivered via the spoken word. Tone and delivery are important to them and they need to *hear* what you are saying. They speak in a more modulated and paced way. You need to use words that are sound related – "That rings a bell", "That resonates with ...", "Echoes of..." and "Hear what I say".

- **Kinaesthetic people**, who are more prepared to accept information that touches them emotionally, through stories that are experiential, that relate to feelings and life situations.

    They speak slowly and use words that are well considered and pondered upon.

    They have to process information so that it *feels* right.

    They need to *feel comfortable* about a situation and the words you use need to reflect this attitude. "How do you feel about this?" "Do you remember a time when ...", "When you reflect back".

QVC The Shopping Channel bases the majority of its presentations, demonstrations and selling calls to actions by making the emotional connection.

Analyse how other TV shows such as The X Factor, Britain's Got Talent and Strictly Come Dancing use emotional 'back stories' and 'struggle to attain' examples. All this to enrol us in the lives and aspirations of other, to make us feel 'this could have been me' and, specifically, to get us to pick up the phone and vote.

In reality you, as a master influencer, should strive to move your audience from their primary modality to the 'feeling' one.

You need to incorporate into your presentations and selling activities all the speech modalities and use pace, tonality and phrasing to engage, re-engage and enrol your audience.

You need to be aware when your audience is switching off, because you are not speaking to them in their language.

Be watchful when the people in the front row or those round the boardroom table are folding or unfolding their arms; if they are leaning in or pushing back. Are their heads nodding in agreement or just nodding off? When there are more yawns than yeses you need to take action.

This information is of immense value when you use these skills to bring about change in a business environment, in a selling situation or to maintain the interest of your audience.

Bear in mind that the proof of effective communication is the positive response you get. It's evidence that your communication and key messages are getting through.

Here we have only scratched the surface of the concept of Neuro Linguistic Programming.

Neuro – An understanding of the brain and how it receives information.

Linguistics - The effective use of targeted language.

Programming – How we are programmed to react to a set of stimuli.

This concept gives you the power of sensory acuity and illustrates how it can make a measurable difference in your ability to communicate effectively.

However, it is a significant first step in enabling you to build instant rapport with everyone that you meet.

Rapport has to be maintained not only at the start of a presentation, but throughout. You have to be constantly aware of your audience, constantly tailoring and tweaking to fit their changing mood. Anything that gets in the way between you and them is a bad thing. PowerPoint is the devil because it creates a wall between you and your audience. It takes their attention away from you and, most importantly, takes your attention and awareness away from them.

Sensibility Warning

In light of the above I am going to say something now that might upset you. Something that when I say it may leave you bereft, unsure or even lost for words. Especially as it's something you may have relied upon all your working life.

It is the equivalent of telling you that the world is not round, but flat; of ordering you to stop eating your favourite food and banning you from ever seeing your most cherished relative again.

So what is this earth shattering, fear inducing, seismic plate shifting request.

Stop using PowerPoint!

Let me qualify that for you. Stop using PowerPoint as your default facility whenever you present your products, ideas, services or concepts.

I'm not saying never use it again. That would be cruel and, frankly, impractical.

No. What I'm saying is decide first whether it is really necessary for you to use it and then combine it with other methodologies to deliver your message and get your point across with power and impact.

Or, if you are brave enough, discard it completely.

Why this seemingly unreasonable request?

Because PowerPoint stands between you and your audience. It stops you from making eye contact and developing the emotional connection essential for your audience to believe in what you are saying.

It stops you from creating the trust needed for them to accompany you on this journey of discovery and knowledge you are going to take them on.

It stops you from using your newly acquired knowledge of sensory perception and completely removes your ability to adapt as you won't even notice that you are losing your audience.

Moreover, when used badly, it is the lazy person's way of presenting.

Death by PowerPoint Reality Check

Picture this – you, as a member of the audience are sitting in a room. The lights are dimmed so you can see the screen that dominates the front of the room even more clearly.

The ceiling mounted projector is humming ominously, hung like a sword of Damocles above your head. Or if it's on a table the cables split the room down the middle.

A huddle of people are hunched over a computer trying to make the machine 'speak' to the projector and the USB key yield the information contained within its microscopic diodes.

All this serves to do is alienate you and the audience, makes everyone impatient and increases the nerves and tension of the presenter.

There's a hush as the screen flickers and at last the first of countless slides fills your vision.

Eventually the speaker starts to talk. Three slides in you're already confused by the morass of lengthy bullet pointed, floated in, faded out and ClipArt information.

By slide five you start to lose the will to live and do what you always do when you're bored, faced with a glimmering screen, in an over warm environment, with dimmed lighting – fall asleep (or, if you've really switched off, start thinking about something else – your next holiday, the end of quarter figures or what's for dinner).

So who is really suffering death by PowerPoint?

Not the audience, they're sleeping peacefully.

It's the presenter.

Why would you inflict this on your audience?

When you let PowerPoint do the driving, you miss a golden opportunity to make the personal and emotional impact needed to be influential. When you are so focused on your slides you are missing the subtle messages the audience is giving off and the sensory awareness to do something about it.

If you're letting PowerPoint get in the way of achieving your presentation goals, here is some help and insights to enable you to make the most of your speaking opportunities.

So, having declared my evangelical message not to use PowerPoint let's start with the 7 Golden Rules that will ensure you don't die at the front of the room when you use it.

In addition, I'll explore some of the questions that I'm often asked.

- What is the significance of the 7 – 10 minute rule?
- What do you do when you are losing the audience's attention?
- How do you get it back?
- How do you press the attention reset button?
- What is a Pattern Interrupt?
- When should you use props?

Especially pay attention to Golden Rule 4. In the following points the advice here works particularly well if you are **not** using PowerPoint and are instead delivering a highly interactive, information rich session.

Remember your objective in presenting is to have a stream of people queuing for more information, wanting your business card and wishing to arrange a 1-2-1 meeting with you at the end.

1: Ask yourself, do I really need to use PowerPoint?

If the answer is Yes, Yes, Yes, regardless of my advice not to use it, here are some hints and tips – if you really must.

PowerPoint can be an exceptional presentation tool when used well, but all too often it acts as an aid memoir to the presenter, rather than a means of delivering valuable and relevant information.

Avoid slides heavy with written content that force your audience to read rather than listen. If you're really concerned (and many people are) that you'll forget what you want to say here are a couple of processes that will help you remember.

Prepare and memorise your content

Firstly, write out your talk in full.

Re-read it and chunk it down to paragraphs.

From those paragraphs identify keywords and place them on a cue card and if necessary keep it in the palm of your hand. You'll be amazed how few times you will actually need to refer to it.

Alternatively, have your key points written down on a piece of paper and, if you feel that you've missed something important out, go ahead and look at it. Tell the audience that this is what you are doing.

Let them know that what you have to tell them is important and you want to make sure you haven't missed anything vital. They'll be more than happy for you to check your notes. It also gives you an opportunity to come 'off script' and reconnect with them.

Mind mapping

An excellent process to aid you in remembering your content, order and flow is Mind Mapping. A concept developed by Tony Buzan, a renowned author and educational consultant.

In his words; "A Mind Map is a powerful graphic technique which aids memory and cortical skills -words, images, numbers, and colours in a single powerful manner. It can be applied in every aspect of life where improved learning and clearer thinking can enhance performance."

2: Find alternatives to PowerPoint

Sure, there's some information that can only be delivered visually, but you don't have to use PowerPoint. Consider how much more effective your visuals would be on a mood board, a flip chart or in a written document handed out to the audience.

If you are referring to a graph, flow chart or have to discuss financial or fiscal information, break away from the formal presentation and distribute the relevant printed sheets.

3: Make yourself the focus of attention

If you really have to use a slide, aim for one that has a picture or is illustrative (remember that PowerPoint is a *visual* aid, not a *verbal* aid). Include slides that have nothing on them, step into the light and regain the attention of your audience.

Or, horror of horrors, turn the bl***dy thing off. Use another illustrative medium – props are memorable – to make your point and turn the computer back on only when it's needed.

4: Engage, re-engage & retain their attention

When you first start your presentation you only have SEVEN SECONDS to get your audience's attention; you then have only 30 seconds to motivate them to listen to you further. Then every 7 – 10 minutes you have to do something to re-engage with them.

You have to hit the *ATTENTION RESET BUTTON*.

You have to do something unexpected, seemingly incongruous, or relate a story or personal experience. If you can, tell a joke (but only if you can do it well). Jokes or amusing anecdotes are a classic tactic speakers use to quickly grab their audiences attention or re-engage with them.

We like people who make us laugh. We are drawn to them because they make us feel good.

WARNING: Be aware that not any old joke will do. It should be relevant to either your subject matter or even better to your audience. The best jokes are relevant to both.

A good joke not only gets a laugh, but positions you as someone who understands your audience and has insight into what they're dealing with.

Client Case Study – Joking with Impact

One client I worked with was asked to give a motivational speech at a networking group for Women in Journalism.

The seminar was attended by editors and reporters from the UK's national and trade media. After her initial opening and about ten minutes into her presentation she told the following joke:

"Barack and Michelle Obama are enjoying a quiet dinner at a local restaurant in Washington. The restaurant's owner approaches the secret service agents and asks if he might have a word with the First Lady.

The agents ask her permission and she agrees. Michelle approaches the owner and the two talk. After a few minutes they share a warm embrace and she returns to her table.

On re-joining her husband Barack asks who the man was. She explains that he is an old flame from college.

Barack says, "Just think honey, if you had married him, you could have been the wife of a restaurant owner."

"No darling," she says, *"If I had married him, he would have been the President of the United States!"*

A good joke in its own right, but on this occasion it was so in-tune with the values of her audience that as she told the punch line, the audience saw it coming and joined in.

It was the perfect attention reset button as it was unexpected and acted as a 'pattern interrupt'. A pattern interrupt is a device that is used by presenters to bring the audience back from being inside their own heads and reconnecting with the speaker.

TOP TIP

The ideal time for a pattern interrupt is when the previous element of the presentation has dealt with a thought provoking or personal issue that the listener has to think through or process.

Bring them back into the room by asking a question such as, 'does that make sense to you?' Seeking a reaction from the audience establishes if they are still with you or whether you have lost their attention or, worse still, alienated them.

By the end of the talk people were thrusting their cards into my client's hand asking her to contact them.

A joke's power is its ability to make your audience feel part of your presentation. The more your audience feels that you understand them, the closer the bond you will create with them.

An alternative to a joke is a story or the use of a prop such as a magazine or newspaper.

Show a copy of the newspaper and read out a relevant passage, preferably one that you have found that day, that makes your point and reinforces your key message.

One executive I worked with was invited to present at a conference on how he had overcome the difficulties of introducing a new reporting and accounting system into his organisation. He illustrated what could have been a very dry topic by using a Russian 'nesting' Doll.

As each doll was revealed he explained the levels of complexity, negotiation and consultation that had to be entered into and overcome. The presentation was roundly acclaimed and resulted in a consultancy with another organisation.

An understanding of your audience will enable you to develop your content and structure your key messages, so that maximum retention is achieved.

Sensory acuity gives you the opportunity to really tune in to your audience and establish whether they are still with you.

- Look for the folded arms at the front of the room.
- Are they taking notes?
- Are they eager to ask questions?
- Are they leaning forward attentively?

Other ways to engage

With the advent of sophisticated software and the higher memory capacity of laptops and other mobile devices it's easy to incorporate video into your slide show, so it really makes an impact.

Even when you are not using slides think how a relevant video can be used. YouTube and the videos you have created are becoming more and more important. It's not about a slick production, it's about the message.

Use music. The relevant song lyric, orchestration or sound track has tremendous emotional weight to create a mood or atmosphere. Note that you may have to gain authority from the performing rights society unless the piece is in the public domain.

Appropriate vivid imagery, not clipart, is another way of keeping your audience interested. If you're intending to use photos of well-known people, choose carefully as you will be judged by the reputation of the people you use and the associations that they have in the minds of your audience.

It is the same with quotations. Use of a relevant quote from a respected and well-known person will elevate what you are saying and, by association, enhance your level of authority

5. No 'Thank You'

One of the mistakes I see too often in a slide or flip chart presentations concerns the last slide or sheet. How many times have we seen it say

THANK YOU for your attention

or

QUESTIONS

or

CONTACT INFORMATION

Consider this; the last piece of information is the one that stays up the longest. It's there while you are answering questions. It's there when you are being thanked for your presentation.

It should contain your key selling message, your eBook, your 'white paper' or your compelling reason for people to do business with you. It does the selling for you so that you don't have to. Every presentation should have a compelling reason built into it – make sure yours is front and centre when your presentation is over.

A very successful executive coach who works with aspirational women that are planning their careers to gain board level positions has this as her last slide.

If you don't plan your life - others will plan it for you.

Here are some examples from major companies that pay thousands of £s to create selling strap lines that you may be able to use too: -

'Just do it'

'Think different'

'Because you're worth it'

'I'm lovin' it'

'It's the real thing'

'Yes we can'

If you can't remember which company these strap lines belong to, the answers are at the end of this chapter.

6: Get your audience writing

Q: How do you know if you are really connecting with your audience?

A: When they do what you ask them to do.

By instructing people to write you are conveying the fact that this information is important, valuable and worth remembering.

When they are writing they are buying, because they are showing you that they also consider what you have shown them to be of value. It tells you that you have got it right and the information you have offered has hit the mark.

Identify who is taking notes as these are the people you should approach after the presentation.

7: Get them discussing

Interaction with your audience is the key to getting the emotional connection you need to gain their buy-in and trust.

If you are using PowerPoint put a challenging statement on the screen to trigger discussion and get the audience to discuss it amongst themselves and then report back their findings.

If you are using a flip chart, place the statement on the board and distribute blank sheets and get the audience to write the ideas on their sheets. Pair them up or get them into small groups and ask them to designate a 'scribe' and another person to present the findings back to the room.

If done well discussion exercises can help identify how the audience feels about a particular challenge and helps to direct the rest of the talk.

Never assume you know what problems your audience is feeling; get them to verbalise them. This will give you the opportunity to tell a story about how you resolved this situation for a client.

Remember, it's not what you do, it's what you have done for others. That's what sells.

Have fun with your presentations. With that in mind, here's an amusing but very informative video of how not to use PowerPoint:

Life After Death by PowerPoint 2012 by Don McMillan:

http://bit.do/DMPP

Key Learning

Have the courage to step away from the projector. Find other ways of delivering your message.

PowerPoint prevents you from connecting with your audience. When focus is on the screen it's not on you and you are giving them the opportunity to switch off.

If you lose eye contact with the people you are speaking to how can you read them and know when you are losing them.

Exercise 4 – Become A Student of People

Write down the words and phrases of the people you come into contact with.

How do they describe their experiences?

Do they speak quickly, in a measured way or are they ponderous?

Do their eyes flick up, to the side or downwards?

Here are those famous strap lines. Did you get them all?
'Just do it' – Nike
'Think different' – Apple
'Because you're worth it' – L'Oreal
'I'm lovin' it' – McDonalds
'It's the real thing' – Coke
'Yes we can' – Presidential Candidate Obama.

Chapter 5

C – CONGRUENCY

What you say, how you say it and how you look when you say it has to be congruent.

In a workshop session I invited a big burly fellow, to help me demonstrate congruency.

As he stepped up to the front, I said "Thank you for volunteering to be my victim, sorry guinea pig, no, I mean helper and trusting me to not to harm you mentally. Are you worried, sorry, nervous, no, <u>happy</u> to work with me on this?"

"Yes" he replied, if a little warily.

"Good," I said and continued "What will happen is that I am going to push against your shoulder and ask you to resist me as best as you can".

My helper nodded.

"Firstly though, I want you to close your eyes and picture a situation when you were feeling depressed: perhaps an argument with someone or a job that you have been putting off that you feel guilty about. Something that gives you an uncomfortable feeling."

My helper obediently closed his eyes and his face assumed a concentrated frown.

I tapped his forehead and watched his body language carefully. His facial expression showed he was thinking of something that made him frown and his breathing had become shallower and slightly quicker. I could see that he was in a negative state.

If he had not shown these signs I would have asked some more negative questions to increase his discomfort. In this case I didn't think this was necessary and I continued with the exercise

"OK, please open your eyes. I am going to push your shoulder. Try and resist me".

When my helper is deep enough into a negative state of mind they are unable to resist me at all and fall away from the shoulder pressure. This big chap clearly tried to resist, but it was easy for me to push his shoulder away until he began to lose his balance and had to step back.

The first part of the exercise was complete, but there was more to come.

I explained, "OK, I am not going to leave you in this negative state. What is going to happen now is I am going to ask you to close your eyes again and visualise a bright positive healing, confidence building light in front of your forehead."

He closed his eyes, but this time there was no frown, just a calm peaceful look on his face. Again I tapped his forehead and continued "This light is now passing down through your chest into your stomach down into your solar *plexus, the centre of your strength and power." He was focused on his visualisation.*

"Now open your eyes, stand firm and resist with all your power and resolve," I instructed. Again I pushed firmly against his shoulder.

He did not budge an inch and, although his shoulder rotated away a little, his feet were fixed and firm and there was never any danger of him losing his balance.

I knew what to expect, but the astonishment on the face of my helper was evidence that he couldn't work out what had happened.

Reality Check

From the moment you take centre stage, rise from your seat to speak or make a presentation to the Board a judgment will be made about you. Even before you open your mouth an assessment of whether it is worth listening to you has been made.

Your currency with your audience, if they have never met you before, is pretty much zero.

It doesn't matter how good your products and services are. It doesn't matter how well you do what you do. And it doesn't matter how highly your clients think of you. If your audience doesn't buy into you, they won't buy into your business or ideas. After all, as the old saying goes, 'people buy people first'.

You have to be CONGRUENT.

What does that mean? The dictionary defines congruency as the state achieved by coming together, the state of agreement, harmony; compatibility. From the Latin congruō meaning "I meet together, I agree".

What does that mean to you?

In terms of our discussion it means that what you say, how you say it and how you look when you say it has to be in harmony.

We will explore four aspects of congruency.

Physical congruency – How your body language ensures that you giving off the right physical message
Mental congruency – How you feel psychologically
Congruency in your appearance – How you ensure your clothes reinforce your message
Verbal congruency – How to ensure you are using the right language and some verbal tricks of the great orators of our time.

Physical congruency

This is all about your physiology. How you walk to the lectern, how you stand, if you fidget, pace about, avert your eyes, or use your hands too much.

I remember the advice I was given by a barrister who coached me on how I should walk to the witness box when I appeared as an expert witness on a property case.

Her recommendation was to walk purposefully to take the stand, open my file, lay out the notes, settle my hands either side of the box, give a courtly nod to the Judge and meet the gaze of the opposing barrister.

Confidence, Authority and Calmness. This is not to impress the opposing barrister, but to impress the Judge. He or she being the only one I needed to convince.

So it is with your colleagues, executives, clients and customers. The messages your physiology or body language sends out; your overall demeanour will be received at a subconscious level.

No longer is it enough to talk the talk you need to walk the walk and embody the essence of your presentation.

However, if you are perceived as unsure, hesitant or lacking in confidence this will be telegraphed to your audience by a myriad of subtle body movements and micro facial expressions.

For your audience to be open minded and be prepared to listen to what you are going to say, then to have it accepted and acted upon, you have to be CONGRUENT.

Initially, the impact you give is non-verbal and there is a misconception that states that 55% is body language, 38% is tonality and only 5% the words you use. This proposition was attributed to Albert Mehrabian Professor Emeritus of Psychology, UCLA, and is a total misreading of his theory.

Of course, words are important. It is only when there is an incongruency or ambiguity between what you say and how you say it that people judge you on your non-verbal message and your emotional state.

It's time to explore the concept of feeling right, looking right and sounding right in the following paragraphs and discover specific exercises to ensure that your message is delivered with power, impact and authenticity.

The first exercise has been designed to develop the right body posture and mental attitude before you take centre stage. It can be used as part of the Mindset section of this book and works on the principle that, if you think that you look good then you feel good. If you feel good then you get good results.

One Point - Mental Preparation

The essence of this process is to clear your mind of the negative voices in your head and instead turn up the volume of the positive ones. Those negative voices may be telling you that you're going to make a fool of yourself, that the content is rubbish and you are going to be tripped up by difficult questions.

Some call this mind over matter.

Remember the story of my helper at the beginning of this chapter? This demonstrates that negative words and negative feelings and situations impact on your mental state and actually physically weaken you.

However, when you think positive thoughts and recall positive situations this strengthens you.

The visualised bright positive light moving from your thinking brain down to your feeling core moves your centre of gravity and enables you to stand firm and appear outwardly strong and mentally confident and prepared.

It is not enough to have the right mind set, to know your objective and that of your audience and having the sensory acuity to of your connection with them.

What you need is to create an air of authority, authenticity and, that word again, TRUST. You need to be CONGRUENT.

Try this exercise for yourself with a friend or colleague. If you tell yourself you are weak and incompetent, you'll experience the physical manifestation of that. If you tell yourself you are strong and ready to face anything, your experience will reflect that.

When you *think* that you embody confidence and authority, then you *feel* you embody confidence and authority.

When you *feel* you embody confidence and authority then you *are* confident and embody authority and get great results.

Does what you wear matter?

Although it is not *all* about the clothes you wear, this does have an impact on the perception people have of you.

During the 16 years I worked with QVC coaching people how to sell on TV we paid special attention to what the individual presenter wore to create the right impression. Unlike face-to-face communication, which happens in the majority of situations, on QVC the guest presenter, who is the perceived expert, does not have any visual clues and verbal feedback. In effect, you are *selling to an invisible audience.*

The only barometer to know how effective you are is if people are picking up the phone to buy.

If the numbers are not ticking over the guest presenter had to adapt their presentations to ensure they were connecting emotionally with the viewers. Their aim was to come across as a person the audience liked and felt had integrity.

At any given point during the presentation, the presenter knew if they had it right by the information being fed to them from the gallery through their earpieces.

The considered attention to what they wore played an important role in that selling presentation and gaining the trust of the viewing public

If they were selling skincare they wore clothes that would be associated with a salon or spa.

If they were selling technology products an open-neck shirt with slacks was appropriate.

Jewellery presenters would wear a smart jacket, tie and immaculate nails for the close ups.

What does this mean to you?

If you are speaking to a room of professionals go suited and booted. You can always remove a tie or a jacket if the majority of the audience is more dressed down. As with the topic and the stories you tell, relevancy in your clothing is the key.

When I work with advertising or PR agencies I will not wear a tie, but I always wear a jacket to maintain an air of authority.

When with sales people I start suited and booted to convey my level of status and then as we get down to work remove my tie, jacket and roll up my sleeves.

I do not want to be prescriptive about what you wear; I am just suggesting that you give it some thought. Is your clothing congruent with what you are selling?

On one occasion I got it completely wrong. Attending a meeting at a major bank I arrived suited and booted to find that it was 'dress down Friday'. Oops! What did I do? Removed my jacket and tie.

Having dealt with the non-verbal aspect of congruency it's time to focus on congruency of speech and the importance of the words and phrases you use.

The words we use have different meanings for different people. This is verbal congruency.

Earlier in this book I told a story about the time I was an estate agent and I learnt how important words are in communicating at a deep physiological level.

I gave the example that when the applicant described to me what they wanted in a property I used their language back to them. I did not paraphrase, I used exactly the same words. This confirmed that I fully understood their needs and was fully engaged in the conversation.

The same applies when presenting in the many business and personal situations you will find yourself in.

Don't use jargon or meaningless acronyms or initials that are known only in your industry. These may create confusion in your audience and you will lose them.

If you really have to use a jargon phrase, qualify it by saying "... which means that ..." or "... commonly known as ..."

It's like using 'street slang', or what I used to know as 'jive talk'. All this does is exclude and alienate your audience.

When presenting, be mindful of the different ways people perceive information, their professional language and phrases and the issues they are facing.

Always talk in terms of the other person's interest and use their phrases. When asked a question from the floor or around the boardroom table seek clarification by saying "To ensure I have fully grasped what you need to know you said ..."

By repeating the question, firstly you gain time to think through your answer and secondly you leave no room for misunderstanding.

In a large gathering repetition of a question enables the audience as a whole to hear the question. Again it gives you more time to craft your answer and it gives the questioner the impression that, by using their exact words, you are in tune with them.

The words people use carry a world of meaning to them and, if you are to maintain congruency, you have to mirror those words and their tonality and pace.

If asked a particularly challenging question often I will tent my fingers. This is when you bring your two hands together as if in prayer. It gives the impression that I am giving the question serious consideration and importance, when in fact I may be praying for divine inspiration and the right words to respond.

Questions from the floor, or around the table during the presentation can be very off-putting and often I hear presenters say that they will park the question until the end of the talk. In my opinion this is wrong.

If a person has a burning question that they feel is essential to their understanding of the points you are making you need to respond. If left unanswered it will leave that individual inside their heads and not following you for the rest of the talk. This means they miss some key points and actions you wish them to take.

Remember, if one person has that question it follows that many others will have the same question that they wish to ask. **So answer it.**

In these circumstances though you have to be adaptable and focused. Keep control, don't get into a protracted discussion or you may disengage the rest of the audience.

If it looks like it is going to be a long discussion. Suggest that you meet with the questioner after the presentation so that you can answer their query in greater depth. Let your audience see that you are making a note of the question. You may want to write it on a flip chart for all to see as this will show that you are taking the questions seriously.

A question that seeks knowledge and clarification of what you are saying may be a buying signal.

Remember when you speak in terms of the audience's needs and concerns that is where your focus is. Rather than keep to your script go with the flow. The result will be more opportunities to do business. You can always get back to the script to make your next point.

There is more about the art of asking questions in the next chapter.

The psychology of language is quite a heavyweight concept and, perhaps, may be off-putting for some of you, so let's lighten the mood.

Let's have a look at some words and phrases that have worked against the speaker.

This is by way of a written 'pattern interrupt'. Do you remember? This mechanism keeps people engaged, listening and receptive. Have you noticed other 'pattern interrupts' I have used in this book?

I have told stories, used conversations, quoted famous people and incorporated pictures. All to maintain your interest.

Here are some examples of verbal **congruency disconnects**.

- Who said "There will be no cover up in the White House"?
- Who made this statement "I did not have sexual relations with that woman"?
- Who continually and vehemently stated - "I'm a natural athlete"?

In contrast here are some examples of absolute congruency.

- I had a dream
- The Lady's not for turning.
- And so, my fellow Americans, ask not what your country can do for you – ask what you can do for your country.

Answers at the end of the chapter and an analysis of why we didn't believe them and why we did.

Congruency Tricks That Gain Buy-In from Your Audience

'Because'.

'Because' is a magic word when you want to get people to do something.

The following is old research, but certainly is worth revisiting as it has absolute relevance for you to effectively influence and persuade others.

It is taken from an article written by Susan Weinschenk Ph.D and relates to research conducted in 1978 by Ellen Langer (Professor of Psychology at Harvard) who published a research study about the power of the word 'because'.

Langer had people request to break in on a queue of people waiting to use a busy copy machine on a college campus. (Remember that this is in the 1970s—there weren't computers and printers. People did a lot more copying at that time, so there were often queues waiting to use a copy machine.

The researchers had the people use three different, carefully worded requests to jump the queue:

- "Excuse me, I have 5 pages. May I use the photocopier?"

- "Excuse me, I have 5 pages. May I use the photocopier, because I have to make copies?"

- "Excuse me, I have 5 pages. May I use the photocopier, because I'm in a rush?"

Did the wording effect whether people let them jump the queue? Here are the results:

- "Excuse me, I have 5 pages. May I use the photocopier?" (60% compliance).

- "Excuse me, I have 5 pages. May I use the photocopier, because I have to make copies?"[93% compliance]

- "Excuse me, I have 5 pages. May I use the photocopier, because I'm in a rush?" [94% compliance]

Using the word 'because' and giving a reason resulted in significantly more compliance. This was true even when the reason was not very compelling ("because I have to make copies").

The researchers hypothesise that people go on 'automatic' behaviour or 'mindlessness' as a form of a short-cut. Hearing the word 'because' followed by a reason (no matter how poor the reason is), causes us to comply.

They also repeated the experiment for a request to copy 20 pages rather than five. In that case, only the "because I'm in a rush" reason resulted in compliance.

What does this mean for you

When you are asking people to try new ideas, accept your propositions or your offering and you feel there may be a level of resistance, use the word 'because'. Then follow this with a compelling reason and you will be amazed how readily they accept.

Embedded Commands

Have you ever wondered how the likes of the late lamented Paul Daniels, an English magician and television presenter and Darren Brown an English mentalist and illusionist were able to influence people to do what they wanted them to do? Hypnotic trance? Not exactly.

Both have stated that their ability isn't supernatural, but through voice tonality, pace and an understanding of how to use language, they can put people in to a receptive mind set.

Sound familiar?

Their skill comes from their deep understanding of how the human brain works, its motivation, behaviour and physiology (that word again). They also incorporate clever use of phrasing, direction and misdirection. These are at the core of most magic tricks.

Without their victims being aware of what is happening they are impelled to carry out tasks and make choices that they have been programmed to make.

One key element is appreciating the fact that our brains cannot process a negative.

So if we ask our children "Don't make a mess". They hear "Make a mess".

If we suggest to our partner "Please don't forget to buy some milk". We are telling them to "forget to buy the milk".

Better to say "Please remember to get some milk" or even better ", "Please remember to get some milk **because** you enjoy white coffee." Both a command and compelling reason to do something that benefits them.

You might find it interesting to watch this video on YouTube.

http://bit.do/DM-DB

Messing With Minds On The London Underground - Derren Brown

Here are some embedded commands that you can use in your presentations: -

"If you are anything like me you will want to ..." *This programs people to like you.*

"You can reject or accept anything I say." *Accept anything I say.*

"No need to write notes as you will recall what I say." *They will recall* and *take notes.*

"Before you consider buying let's talk about the benefits, so you can make the right decision. That way you can buy with confidence". *Multiple commands to **BUY.***

One of the greatest orators of the 20th century was Winston Churchill. Let's look at some of his amazingly well-crafted phrases and look for those emotionally charged embedded commands.

"We shall defend our island, whatever the cost may be, we shall fight on the beaches, we shall fight on the landing grounds, we shall fight in the fields and in the streets, we shall fight in the hills; we shall never surrender."

Here Churchill has used a number of devices. As with Martin Luther King he has used repetition - "We shall fight …" He has drawn a picture of England's 'green and pleasant land' and our role in defending our home. Should the invasion have taken place you can rest assured we would never have surrendered.

Some people may feel uncomfortable using such devices. Let me refer you back to my original proposition.

'To **positively influence** others **to be happy** to take the action we desire them to take.

Key Learning

What you say, how you say it and how you look when you say has to be congruent. It determines whether your audience buys into what you are selling or rejects it.

Lack of response may be because they feel at a psychological level something just does not feel right, sound right or appear in harmony.

Here are the answers to the verbal **congruency disconnects**.

- Who said "There will be no cover up in the White House"? Richard Nixon – He was known as Tricky Dickie and always looked swarthy and needing a shave. Congruent in his use of words and the delivery of those words but not in how he looked.

- Who made this statement "I did not have sexual relations with that women"? Bill Clinton – So congruent in much of his interactions but subconsciously we picked up on the micro facial expressions and body language.

Here are the answers to the examples of **absolute congruency**.

- I had a dream – **Martin Luther King** – His passion, his use of words and voice tonality all were absolutely congruent.

- The Lady's not for turning. – Margaret Thatcher – Accepting that she was not universally respected she also had absolute conviction in her voice, her body language was like Churchill and what she said she would do she did.

- And so, my fellow Americans, ask not what your country can do for you – ask what you can do for your country. – **John F Kennedy** –An impressive looking young man whose charisma shone through and whose style of delivery and words were eloquent and inclusive.

Exercise 5 – Listen To Your Own Self Talk And Create Congruent Phrases For Others

Mentally prepare yourself for your interactions with others.

Following on from Exercise 4, construct phrases that tap into your knowledge of how people perceive information.

Incorporate embedded phrases into your everyday language in both business and personal situations and note the reactions.

Chapter 6

O – ORDER

Take me on a journey of discovery and I will follow you.

"I think it's going to be a momentous flop, I feel very depressed about it. I don't know what else I can do. Essentially, it's a kid's film, but it's not right."

George had just shown to a group of friends and fellow film makers the rough cut of his new film. He wanted to convey the overall concept and had used a mixture of stock World War II battle scenes interspersed with colour scenes filmed on green screen background. There were little or no special effects.

The group of friends, who included Francis Ford Coppola, Martin Scorsese, Steven Spielberg and Brian de Palma decamped to a Chinese Restaurant to discuss the film further.

Everyone was saying things like "Oh, I don't know, it may not work."

The only positive voice came from Steven Spielberg, who rightly predicted the movie would be a hit.

Brian de Palma was really damning. "I don't understand what it was all about. Who's the hairy guy? Who are these people, where do they come from? What's the back story? What is the context?"

George went redder and redder, but out of all this negativity something great came.

Brian suggested "Why don't you do what they did in the old-fashioned movies like Flash Gordon and write a foreword?"

And so he created the iconic scrolling letters disappearing into the far distance

'A long time ago in a galaxy far, far away …'

Still, George Lucas was so convinced that Star Wars would flop that on 25th May, the day it was released, he went on holiday to Hawaii instead of attending the premiere.

*The rest is history, but the lesson for us to learn today is that **Order** is essential. You need to grab the attention of your audience immediately, you need to continually re-engage, motivate and tell your story to make your point.*

So,

- How do you begin your presentation with power and impact so that your audience is immediately engaged?

- How do you order your content so that it flows seamlessly from one topic to the next?

- How do you construct stories that are relevant and enhance your key messages?

- How do you keep your audience entertained, continually engaged and enlightened?

- How do you end your presentation with a clear and specific call to action?

- How do you get a line of people wanting to speak and work with you after your presentation?

This chapter will answer these and other important questions.

How do you begin?

The first moments with your audience are critical. Forget about the effort that's gone into preparing your presentation or the value of the content you have to share. You have about 30 seconds – in fact, some will say you only have SEVEN seconds to make a good first impression.

What you do next will decide whether you'll have your audience's undivided attention or if they'll spend your talk thinking about the workload piling up on their desk, the dinner waiting for them at home or anything else that's on their mind.

Whether you are an invited speaker at a conference or presenting to your colleagues, how you start is essential in changing their perception of what is going to come next and who you are.

As any film star, comedian or musician will tell you, audiences are fickle. Give them what they want and they'll love you forever. Don't and they'll switch off both physically and mentally.

Whether they are watching a film, a stage play, attending a seminar or a meeting, an audience has one thing in common. They want to be entertained and they're looking to you to provide that entertainment. Not that they're expecting you to get up and sing a song or juggle with fire, but they do want to know that they'll enjoy their time with you.

When considering how you are going to open your presentation your personal impact is paramount.

You are already aware that how you look and sound is important and looking fresh and relaxed with an air of confidence will create instant appeal.

~Your audience is looking to you for insight and, to a certain extent, leadership. If you lack confidence or if there's a sense that you're not absolutely sure of what you're saying, your audience will struggle to take you seriously.

However, no matter how well presented you are or how confidently you present, you still have to pull your audience into your talk immediately. Once their attention has wandered it's very difficult to reclaim it.

To get their undivided attention you have to make an entrance. That means immediately hitting them with something that will capture their imagination and have them eager to know what's coming next.

In any situation when you are presenting always, **always get introduced and invited to the front of the room.** Many speakers make the mistake of hanging around just 'off stage' looking like a spare date at a party. Walk purposely from the side of the room or from the back, if that is possible, and take centre stage.

TOP TIP

Find out what introduction the host or your colleague has prepared about you and if you feel it is not powerful enough prepare one in advance and ask them to deliver that.

If you tell people how great you are and what you have accomplished that's bragging. When others do the same it gives you authority and authenticity.

So, you have arrived at the front of the room.

Firstly, thank your host for their generous introduction. Always thank your host. If appropriate also thank or compliment your audience.

You can use phrases like:

"I really appreciate the opportunity of sharing some new ideas with you". Or

"Thanks for letting me interrupt your breakfast/lunchtime/evening to share some new ideas with you".

You can even butter them up a little by saying,

"There is a tremendous amount of talent/knowledge/ experience in the room and it's great to have the opportunity to discuss the topic I want to share with you".

Never thank them for their valuable time or taking time out to listen to you. Your time is just as important and precious as theirs.

A typical opening I use is a bit jokey and cheesy, but in my QVC days cheesy always worked for me.

When I get introduced to the front of the room in the way I have just suggested it is often to a round of applause.

I say: "You know it always amazes me how generous an audience is by clapping before they even know what they are going to get, so thank you".

Notice the embedded commands. I'm telling them they are going to be **amazed** and they are going to be **generous** to me.

The objective here is always to engage the audience immediately. To make them feel that something out of the ordinary is going to happen, even if you're presenting to people who know you. Doing something different changes their perceptions of you.

State a SHOCKING STATISTIC

It has to be relevant to that audience. If I am speaking to an audience say of retailers I might say: "A recent study showed celebrity endorsements have zero effect." I might add. "However, if a male actor, who matches the endorsed product, expresses his endorsement by actively using it, there might be a value. The reality is that quality customer service is the real star".

This opens the door for a discussion about the value of great sales people and how the best have the ability to create great personal relationships.

Relate a PERSONAL EXPERIENCE

This will be something that makes a business point or gives you credibility and authority.

I might talk about my time with QVC coaching guest presenters how to sell in that TV environment. How they are selling to an invisible audience and the importance of knowing their audience.

How actors were the worst to coach as they viewed the presentation as a role and came across as false to the viewing public. Whereas people who had a genuine passion for the product had an air of authenticity and were able to sell substantially more.

This gives me credibility and by name-dropping an association with a major retailer, provides an insight into my coaching style and a sophisticated transition into my talk on sales and pitching.

Make a MYSTERIOUS STATEMENT

This may cause confusion, but is a device to grab the attention. An example:

I will ask the audience "Before I start talking about the specific topic of … let me ask you. Are you happy to come on a mystery journey with me"? Hopefully, I get a few nodding heads.

"I would like you to imagine you are walking through a woodland; it's autumn and the leaves are slowly floating to the forest floor. You are walking through the leaves and they are making that wonderful noise autumn leaves make. But, instead of leaves its paper. Now what is the normal colour of paper?"

"White", comes the reply.

"Now let me take to you to the top of Whistler Mountain and the snow is all around us and people are throwing snowballs. Now what is the normal colour of snow?" "

White". is the reply again.

"Now, what do cows drink?"

"Milk", the majority of replies come from the audience. Then after a short pause people then correct themselves, "No, water".

I smile "Of course it's water"

"Isn't it interesting that by painting pictures for you and asking you to step into them with me. I can get you to say what I want you to say?"

I'm then into my talk. Being sold to is no longer effective, but persuasion and influence are the way forward.

Use a QUOTE by a famous person that will pique interest

"I have always said that everyone is in sales. Maybe you don't hold the title of salesperson, but if the business you are in requires you to deal with people, you, my friend, are in sales.

Zig Ziglar

By using a quote from a famous person, it elevates your authenticity and adds validity to the topic you are going to speak on.

The key here is always to make it relevant and meaningful to the audience. At best it draws a picture that they can step into.

"If your actions inspire others to dream more, learn more, do more and become more, you are a leader".

John Quincy Adams – American President.

If appropriate you can read out a testimonial provided that it illustrates not what you do, but what you have achieved for others.

TELL A JOKE

Not everyone feels comfortable telling a joke. Nor is it always relevant or appropriate to do so. If it does not come naturally, don't do it.

Here's a joke I have used in different situations:

A woman finds Aladdin's magic lamp. She starts rubbing it and a Genie appears.

The woman looks at the Genie and asks him to grant her the following wishes:

"I want my husband to have eyes only for me"

"I want to be the only one in his life"

"I want that when he gets up in the morning I'm the first thing he grabs and takes me everywhere he goes."

The Genie turned the lady into an iPhone.

Be aware that if you have a predominately female audience you may need to change the genders in the story.

I've used this joke as a lead into:

- How technology is taking over our lives
- How we are losing the art of verbal communication
- An awareness that our marketing and messaging must be mobile friendly.

Do something surprising

Anyone familiar with the comedy genius that was Morecambe and Wise will be aware of the power of surprising your audience. With Eric and Ernie you never knew what was going to happen, which is what made them so engaging. The opening of their TV shows were always highly anticipated. Ernie would play it straight and we would hold our breaths waiting for Eric's entrance.

Not that you need to do something funny. Creating surprise is about doing something unexpected that grabs the interest of your audience.

We were at a networking event where the speaker was talking about mentoring. He came onto the stage and before he addressed the audience for the first time, he walked up to the flip chart and on the blank page wrote in large red letters,

£1,000,000

Turning to the audience, he said in a very confident tone, "this is how much money I'm going to make for you." Suffice to say he had their undivided attention after that.

Use music

Come on to music or introduce it into your presentation at key points

There's a reason why boxers enter the ring to an upbeat and exciting theme; it creates energy and excitement in the room.
Sure the audience is already pumped, but the music helps increase anticipation and focus them on the main event.

Creating the right emotional connection with the audience is important because people decide logically, but buy emotionally. We need to ensure that what we say and do taps into both elements of that equation.

When you set the right emotional tone, you are already much closer to a sale. Music is a good way of setting the emotional charge of your presentation right from the start. Yes, you've got to maintain that charge once you're on stage, but those that do will have their audience eating out of the palm of their hands.

Whatever methods you decide to make an initial impact, keep on reinforcing that impact, remember your job is to capture the imagination of your audience so that they can't help but stay attentive and focused on what you're saying.

Ordering your content

How do you order your content so that it flows seamlessly from one topic to the next?

During my 16 years as Chief Guest Presenter Coach for QVC I developed a framework that could be adapted for any selling presentation. Whether it was a computer, technology, a piece of jewellery or kitchen cleaning products.

The process is called **THE 4 CORNERSTONES OF A WINNING PRESENTATION**.

This is the same framework that I use when coaching Executives, Sales Directors and others to enable them to sell their concepts, projects and ideas.

1: PERSONAL CREDIBILITY

What right do you have to talk about the product, service or proposition you are offering?

Your position and time with the company.

Your leadership credentials.

Your creative input or how you have used the product or service.

2: COMPANY CREDIBILITY

The history of the organisation.

Your departmental successes.

The quality of the item, methods of production, evolution of design or level or service that the company gives to your clients.

3: THE FACTS ABOUT THE PRODUCT

The detail of what the product, proposition, service offers.

Some specific figures on the impact on the bottom line, percentage increase on turnover, value it brings or how it performs, what it is made from.

4/5 key features that are indisputable.

4: WHAT THAT MEANS TO ME/THEM -

The stories behind the design

The experiences of your customers, client or individuals both emotional and aspirational.

Not only features and benefits, but what your prospect's colleagues or Executive will experience when they buy what you are selling.

What's In it For Me and them.

Pressing the Attention Reset Button

REMEMBER THE 7 – 10 MINUTE RULE

Your audience is now listening attentively, having been warmed up and regaled with compelling stories. They are anticipating further interesting, informative and hopefully entertaining anecdotes and relevant information.

You've thanked the person who introduced you and thanked the audience. You've started with impact, outlined what you are going to talk about and offered some credibility statements that validates your **RIGHT TO TALK**.

Not what you have done, but what you have done for others.

You're into the main 'meat 'of your topic and if you have been talking for around 10 minutes it's time to do something to reengage the audience.

Here are a couple of ways to do this.

Get Them Involved

You need to get your audience not only mentally involved and listening to your presentation, but physically involved and active.

Although this may feel a bit daunting to some, when you get your audience involved you create energy, enthusiasm and emotion. All three of which are ideal for grabbing and maintaining engagement and attention.

Ask them a question that requires a show of hands. Not only will they feel duty bound to respond (you've got to love the programming we get at school), but it also presents a risk-free way for audience members to be noticed.

It will make them feel special and give them a stronger sense of belonging in the room.

This is a good opportunity to find out exactly who's in the room with you. This has two positive effects.

> You can ensure whatever information you've prepared is tailored exactly to their needs

> They'll feel like you're taking an interest in them.

Depending on the size of the group you may want to write their individual responses on a flip chart.

Make sure to tell them why you want the information. People like to know what's happening to them and will appreciate your making the talk specific to their needs.

Use A Prop

Props can transform your presentation and make it memorable, talked about and enhance your key message. The prop you choose must always be relevant to your topic and make a specific point.

Often, I scour the daily newspapers to find an article that reinforces a point that I want to make.

- If I am discussing how in every area of our lives trust is lacking, I find an article that illustrates this.

- If I want to show how we are enrolled by emotionally charged stories, I will identify a story that show this.

Newspaper articles are great to add credibility and authenticity to your argument and shows that you are up-to-the-minute in your thinking.

At some point in my presentation when I feel that either I am losing my audience, need to ensure that they have 'got' the key points of my talk or after I have discussed a particularly intense or weighty concept I use **The Umbrella Trick**.

It goes like this:

I say, "We've been talking about a serious and complex issue and I feel it's about time we have some fun." I then reveal a pocket size umbrella that up until this point has been hidden.

"Can I ask is anybody superstitious as I am going to open this umbrella?

"Never mind, I'm going to open it anyway"

I then go into the sell.

"Have you ever been in a situation where you have started out on your journey with blue skies, then got out of the tube or jumped off the bus, to find that it's pouring?

"Not wanting to get soaked you go to one of those street vendors or nip into Boots and buy the first umbrella you lay your hands on.

"You then step out into the street, a gust of wind picks up and blows your newly bought umbrella inside out. The spokes bend and it's useless.

"Well, with this umbrella it won't happen". I then open it up and it expands to a full height, full width umbrella. I show that it has a vent that allows the wind to pass through and prevents it from blowing inside out to gusts of up to 30 mph.

"It is also Teflon coated which means that the rain just beads off. You give it a shake, and it's almost dry so that you can put it in your pocket, briefcase, or back into your handbag".

The presentation is greeted with laughter and requests of "where can we buy one?"

I explain that when I presented it on QVC in the space of just 7 minutes I regularly sold over a thousand pieces, at the cost of £21.50. The value of which equates to around £3,000 per minute.

I ask "How many of us would like to earn £3, 000 per minute?"

I then ask "Why would I have at this point of my presentation brought out this umbrella?"

Various replies come back and I explain the following reasons:

> First of all it's an attention reset button to reengage with them.

> It illustrates an experience that many of us have had and is an illustration of the PAIN to PLEASURE concept

> It is an emotionally charged story

> It has been told in the space of no more than 2 minutes, a key amount of time to tell an engaging story.

> It reinforces and aids recall of the key messages I have presented to that point in the talk

Here are 6 rules to use props effectively

1. Use them when they are least expected
2. Make an emotional connection
3. Use them to tell an encapsulated story
4. Practice using them
5. Make it memorable
6. Make it relevant.

Once you have finished using the prop put it away. Fiddling with it is distracting and takes away for what you will do next.

Here is another example how the use of a prop enhanced the presentation of a person that had always been thought of as a mediocre presenter - Bill Gates

Bill Gates and the Mosquitos Prop

That perception changed when in 2009 he unleashed one of the most memorable props ever on his audience: live mosquitos.

About a third of the way through his TED talk titled Mosquitos, Malaria, and Education, Gates did the unthinkable. He lifted up a glass jar, and let mosquitos loose in the lecture hall, saying:

"Now, malaria is, of course, transmitted by mosquitos. I brought some here, just so you could experience this. We'll let those roam around the auditorium a little bit. (Laughter) There's no reason only poor people should have the experience. (Laughter) (Applause).

Those mosquitos are not infected."

His prop was perfect: tightly related to his core message, concrete (not abstract), unexpected, humorous, and entirely memorable.

While a single prop did not transform him from a mediocre presenter to a dynamic presenter in an instant, there's no question that his presentation benefited greatly from this inspired prop.

Now we come to another most important element of your presentation.

The Close

How you end the presentation is as important as the opening.

You already know that, if you are using PowerPoint or a flip chart, the last slide or sheet should have your key message emblazoned as large as possible on it. It will be the last piece of information they see and will remain in their eye line all the time you are answering their questions.

Make it strong, emotional and relevant. It should reinforce something you have said before and works on the basis of the golden rule of sales:

> *Tell them what you are going to tell them,*
>
> *Tell them,*
>
> *Then tell them what you've told them.*

A good salesperson encourages their prospects to take positive action that leads to a mutually beneficial outcome. If all goes well this sequence concludes with signatures on a contract and the provision of services that enable the buyer to achieve their goals and the seller to add profit to their bottom line.

Like any sales activity, the conference or seminar talk is just one step in a sequence of interactions that drives the prospect from one sales milestone to the next.

Don't be fooled into thinking that your presentation should take the audience from interested party to signed customer. Your talk is more akin to a cold call than a close. For most it is an opportunity to start building awareness of your business and the credibility that you are an expert at what you do.

The goal should be to encourage a desire for further interaction in a private setting, where you can have one-to-one time with your prospect.

Triggers are a means by which to drive further interaction. Here are three that work very well.

Special Report

There is only so much you can cover in a seminar or conference talk. When done well, you should have answered some of the questions your audience members had when they arrived, but also you will have left them wanting more.

Not everybody is going to feel comfortable coming up to you after your talk.

Offering further information in the form of a special report that can be downloaded from your website is an excellent tactic for triggering further interaction.

It also gives you a means to get their email address and get them to opt in to receiving more information from you in the future via a blog or newsletter.

Seminar

The next interaction you have with your audience doesn't have to be free. In fact, if you have done your job properly, they will be chomping at the bit to get more information from you and willing to pay to get it.

Organising your own seminar that people pay to attend enables you to build revenue, spend more time with your prospects and identify those people that are most likely to do business with you.

Prize Draw

If you are speaking to a group of business people, offer an hour's free consultancy via a business card draw. That way you get a meeting and bunch of cards to follow up on.

You could also take this a stage further. Invite your audience to download the special report on your website and award a free consulting session to the first five people who download the report.

Scarcity and competition are powerful drivers of behaviour. Offering a limited number of sessions will almost certainly ensure you have interest.

Top Tips

Watch closely the people who are asking questions. A question is a buying signal and you should ask their name so that you can go up to them after you have finished your talk. Get their cards and let them know that you will contact them.

The success of your talk can be measured by the number of people waiting to speak to you once you have left the stage.

Exercise 6 – Decide What Props, Articles and Appropriate Jokes You Will Use

Scour the newspapers and online for articles, blogs and tweets that support your subject.

Create an arsenal of relevant humorous stories, jokes or quotes that enhance your own words.

What props can you use as an 'attention reset button', that are relevant and interesting?

Chapter 7

W – WORK THE ROOM

-----❖-----

Your presentation is not the end, it's the beginning.

I was asked by The College of Occupational Therapists to present a keynote speech on how to build an effective business by gaining referrals and attending networking events.

Prior to the event I spent a considerable amount of time speaking to the organisers. This helped me to understand the problems that OTs experience in their businesses and the challenges of working with hospitals and doctor's surgeries.

As OTs they are highly qualified in their profession, but not in terms of their business activities.

My niece, who is an OT, told me a number of stories of her experiences that I could bring in to my talk. A lesson here is that if you don't have specific knowledge of a sector and don't have relevant stories, get them from others. Ensure that you give due credit to your sources.

Getting to the conference early, during one of the breaks, I made my way around the room and sat at the various tables. I asked my pre-prepared questions and noted their replies and their names, ensuring that I got their OK to use both.

One lady I remember very quizzically and, I think, jokingly asked, "Are you asking these questions so you can go away and write your presentation now"?

I responded, "Actually yes. I know what I want to talk about, but I want to tailor it so that it is really meaningful for you".

The presentation went extremely well. Questions from the floor flowed and, as I left the stage, a number of business cards were thrust into my hands with requests for me to speak to them for further advice and help.

The comments I received post the conference included these:

> *"He stood out as excellent particularly as he visited tables beforehand and engaged with us personally rather than talking at us".*

> *"Excellent and relevant".*

> *"Very interesting and useful tips to engage people who I want to work with".*

Key Learning

When you make direct and personal contact, have the names of specific individuals and use the knowledge gained of their particular problems. You, as a presenter, and the presentation itself becomes compelling, relevant and emotionally connected.

So now you appreciate how important it is to find out exactly what is causing your prospects, colleagues, clients or customers aggravation, anxiety, fear, worry and PAIN. If you've taken this to heart you will have carried out research, sent out questionnaires, spoken to the organisers of the conference or taken a straw poll from your colleagues to gain these insights.

You know that these insights are the key to a great presentation. One that achieves each party's objective and leaves no shadow of a doubt what they can get out of the interaction.

Let's revisit this principle, but this time look at it from a different perspective.

Now that you are in the room you have a golden opportunity to build on your findings by speaking to the delegates directly.

This may be glaringly obvious, but there are a number of other major advantages to having this direct interaction.

Breaking Down Barriers

As an expert in your field, an authority on your topic, a keynote speaker invited to enlighten, motivate and inspire the gathering throng, delegates may feel that you are aloof or unapproachable.

There are certainly times when this approach would be valid, but when you are selling (using that word in its broadest terms) being on a pedestal will not create engagement. For your audience to buy what you're offering you need to get 'up close and personal'.

By interacting directly with your audience, before your presentation, you will gain a high level of acceptance for you personally and, by association, for the proposition you will be presenting.

By breaking down what, in theatrical terms, is called the 'fourth wall', you close the distance between you as the presenter and your audience. It enables you to connect as a person.

When selling on QVC it was important for the presenter to break down this fourth wall. In TV this is the screen; on a platform or standing at the front of the room, it's the invisible barrier between presenter and audience.

QVC presenters were taught to make the viewer feel that they were sitting alongside them in their own homes. Or, alternatively, that they were part of the action in the studio.

The studios were especially designed to feel like rooms in their homes, in their gardens or at fashion shows so that they could be transported to sit alongside us and join us in our conversation.

It is the same at the theatre where the audience will 'suspend their disbelief' that they are in fact sitting in an auditorium. As they get caught up in the drama and, emotionally, they join the actors in the experience.

Suspension of disbelief has been defined as a willingness to suspend one's critical faculties and believe the unbelievable; sacrifice of realism and logic for the sake of enjoyment.

So it must be with you as a presenter. You must enable the audience to suspend their analysis of your motives and, rather than thinking they are being sold to, believe that they are being enlightened and are making an informed decision to move forward with your project, product, service or idea.

Here are the touchpoints for you to build the foundation for this:

Arrive early

If possible, get a guest list.

Display your name badge high up on your clothes so that it is easily seen and make your way into the melee of people and introduce yourself as the speaker.

You may end up standing beside them with a coffee cup in hand, taking a seat alongside them or sitting chatting at their table.

Get them involved

Explain that it is very important for you to make your presentation as relevant to their needs as possible. Say that you really appreciate if they would tell you what are the burning issues that they would like you to address.

Note their names and ask their permission to refer to your conversation in your presentation.

Depending on the number of people in the room, gaining about five or six attributable comments should be sufficient to confirm the needs of the group as a whole.

In any event speak to as many people as possible, because from the comments obtained you can choose the ones that support your topic.

Even when you are presenting to your colleagues, a customer or client that you know well, gaining confirmation of the issues they are facing reinforces your research, gives you confidence and creates a feeling for them that instead of being sold to they are going to be consulted.

Get them in *your* room

In a situation where you are giving a talk at a conference, where there are number of presentations being made at the same time, it will all be about getting people into *your* room.

There is nothing so frustrating as speaking to a small group when you know others are piling them in.

Getting to speak to as many people as possible during the coffee or meal breaks is an excellent way of helping them to choose your presentation. Ask what their problems are and offer a compelling reason for them to attend your talk. Involvement creates commitment.

You may want to produce a flyer identifying some of the issues you will be resolving for the delegates. If possible take your colleagues with you so that they can work the room with you.

Give them star billing

Having spoken to some of the delegates, identify them by name during the presentation. Refer to your conversation and the insights gained and, in doing so, you close the gap between you as a presenter and them as an audience.

'People buy people first'

I worked on a presentation with a client who was invited to speak at a major symposium on financing and procurement for Local Authorities. It was very well attended and we had some heavy hitters speaking in other rooms at the same time as my client.

We prepared a flyer identifying the three key issues we knew the Councils were facing. Lack of resources, budget cuts and pressure from Government (nothing new here, then).

My client's presentation identified where money could be clawed back from unclaimed rebates, payments for invoices that had been charged multiple times and accounting errors that had been made.

He had developed a process that would interrogate their accounting systems, identify where duplicate payments had been made and reclaim monies that would reduce at least some of their budgetary shortfall.

This was illustrated in our flyer by a 'pot of gold' at the end of a rainbow. We did not go as far as suggesting that we were leprechauns.

We filled the room.

Get Physical.

In any presentation it is important to project to your audience a feeling of confidence, passion and focus. Whether you are speaking to your Board around a table or to a large gathering at a conference, the energy and physicality you demonstrate will be the difference between success and failure.

You need to keep your audience involved. It is not just about the content, it is most assuredly about the delivery.

Here are some ideas to keep your audience on their toes and you enthusiastic at the front of the room.

There is a principle coined by Tony Robbins an American motivational speaker and self-help guru that states ***Motion Creates Emotion.***

You know that when you are active and move your body, when you exercise, go for a walk, dance or take part in a Pilates or yoga class, you feel energised and the endorphins kick in. Known as the body's natural feel-good chemical, this endorphin kick not only stimulates us, it also stimulates those observing us.

In terms of a presentation, I'm not suggesting you dance around or do press ups, I am suggesting that you should be animated and dynamic.

- If you're behind a podium or lectern, use your body to express your emotions and if it is natural for you to do so use your hands

- If you are really brave, get out from behind the lectern and use the whole of the stage

- If you are on a raised platform or dais, step off it and move down into the body of the room and really make contact with the audience

- If you're seated at a boardroom table stand up and go to the whiteboard, flip chart or smartboard and write something that makes your point.

The great orators and motivators of our time are animated, enthusiastic and totally absorbed in getting us excited about what they are speaking about.

Here are some excellent examples of passion, authenticity and focus.

Michelle Obama American First Lady	http://bit.do/DMMO
Zig Ziglar American Author, Sales Guru	http://bit.do/DMZZ
Simon Sinek British author and marketing consultant	http://bit.do/DMSS

In previous chapters I have made the case for coming away from using PowerPoint and opting for other means of presenting such as a flip chart or printed information that can be tabled during the presentation.

Flip Charts

Flip charts are a great way of demonstrating the concept of motion creating emotion. When you are writing something down there is a dynamic interaction, especially when you have asked for input from the audience.

Drawing a framework and then adding to it element by element without recourse to notes indicates an in-depth knowledge of your subject rather than fading in each piece of information slide by slide.

Top Tip

Use 2 flip charts, one either side of you. On the left write the problems you are addressing and on the right-hand flip chart write the solution. Remember the positioning is from the audience's perspective when you have your back to them.

There is a subliminal message to this positioning. Who is the person standing in the middle of the charts?

The person resolving the problem and offering a solution – YOU.

You can also adopt this methodology in a pitching meeting or one where you are addressing a difficult issue. Take a pad, draw a line down the centre of the page and on the left write 'Problem' and on the right 'Solution'.

Printed Material

On many occasions I have seen presenters displaying PowerPoint slides showing complex information, graphs, flow charts and financial analysis. All much too small for people to read.

In these situations print the information out and distribute it at the appropriate time. Never do this at the beginning of the session as people will read ahead of you and ask questions that may take you off track.

Work Books

This is also true of work sheets. Only distribute them at the point you are actually going to work through them.

The advantage is that, if they already have them in their hands you have to use them. If you decide that they are not relevant to the direction the discussion has taken then you don't have to reference them and the group will not feel that they have been short changed.

Layout of Your Room

There are several options for how your room is laid out.

Theatre Style

This layout is generally used when there is a substantial number of people attending. Video screens may have to be incorporated if the symposium or conference is to be filmed or streamed. Presentations are made from a raised platform or stage and your image is displayed larger than life.

Although you may have little input about the actual layout you can still determine whether you use a hand held microphone (mic), one that fits on your lapel (sometimes known as a lavalier) or a headset. You may also be asked to use a mic on a stand.

When it comes to being in motion, using your hands and connecting with the audience, your choice of mic will have an impact. I prefer a lapel mic or headset as it gives freedom of movement. If you want to leave the stage and get close to your audience, make sure the organisers know when you are going to do that so that the cameras can follow you and the sound engineer can prevent feedback from the loudspeakers.

Cabaret Style

Sitting people in groups at round tables is my one of my favourite layouts as it gives the audience a table to make note-taking easy and, if they are taking notes, they are listening.

It is less formal than theatre style and it encourages communication with others around the table. This is especially advantageous if you are asking the delegates to participate in the presentation. Remember what we said about how to maintain engagement by getting them to do something?

It also allows you to circulate around the tables and, when questions are asked, to direct your answer to the individual questioner.

Boardroom

I like boardroom style too, again it makes note-taking easy. However, it's only suitable with smaller groups and is limited by the size of the room – if you're too far from your audience members in a relatively intimate environment, they can disconnect.

Questions

Questions are the key indicators of how your presentation has been received. The more questions you are asked, the better buy-in you have got.

Asking for questions is also an art. Never, never ask "Has anybody got a question?", it is impersonal and weak. Ask instead, "Who has the first question?" Then give the audience three seconds or so to fill the silence.

It is a very strange phenomenon that we humans do not like silence. In negotiations it is said that he who breaks the silence is in the weaker position. It is also true when asking for questions.

However, you have to keep your nerve. If no questions come from the floor revert to the conversation you had with the delegates when you worked the room.

In addition, have two or three questions prepared that you know people often ask. Here are some I use when needed:

"Typically I am asked … " or

"Many times I have been asked … " or

"One question I was asked when I was talking to you before I stepped on stage was … "

Never get into a protracted debate with one person. This is boring to watch, seemingly disregards others in the room and may get quite heated.

If you're challenged by a disruptive individual who is more interested in hearing their own voice rather than listening to the pearls of wisdom you are conveying I recommend a process called

DISAGREEING AGREEABLY

This is a two-stage process – first thinking, then speaking.

It is relevant when you are pitching or presenting to the Board, your team or colleagues.

Obviously, you should not tell the questioner outright that they are wrong or misguided when they express an opinion. Therefore, you need a process that enables you to consider the answer to the question, offer a compelling example and then deliver it in an effective way.

If you receive a response that challenges the example given you will then need to argue your point without discounting the other person's opinion.

HOT TIP

Avoid using the words BUT or HOWEVER (However is a posh way of saying BUT) as it negates the other persons point of view.

How many times have we heard an interview on TV or radio when in answer to a point made the responder says YES - BUT. Keep the 'but' out of the discussion.

"What would you say if I told you I have met your partner and they are a lovely person BUT......"

Your focus would not be on the 'lovely person', you would focus on the BUT and what I am about to say.

You need to find alternative words to 'but' or 'however'. Words that 'cushion' your response, acknowledge the other person's point of view without discounting it and enable you to make your next point.

Let's use as a specific example of a debatable issue:

24 hour news reporting creates a state of fear.

THINKING: What's my point of view?

WHAT DO I THINK – Breaking news is based on supposition rather than fact

WHY DO I THINK THAT – Because we see all the time the TV channels filling in hard news information with opinions of experts.

AN EXAMPLE - Watch the coverage of any tragic event. The news team rush to the spot and interview anybody with an opinion, whether they are involved or not.

SPEAKING – My point of view is

ONE EXAMPLE IS – Watch the coverage of any tragic event. The news team rush to the spot and interview anybody with an opinion, whether they are involved or not.

THIS EXAMPLE SHOWS – That they are heightening our fears by offering opinions and half-truths rather than facts

THEREFORE I THINK THAT - 24 hour news reporting creates a state of fear

The Opposing View (Encapsulated)

In a fast moving society where knowledge and information is power we need to understand the situation so that we can make valid judgements for the benefit of us our company and our people.

I could respond by saying YES BUT.

Let's try a different way and CUSHION our reply.

CUSHION PHRASES - I accept your point of view, there is another way of looking at it ……….or

That's a valid comment, my view is……..

OK, fair point, have you considered this though………

Choose you own issues and try this process out on friends and family. How many times do they revert to 'yes, but' and 'however'?

Exercise 7 – What Is Happening in Your Prospects World?

Relevancy is the key to connecting with your audience and understanding their pain. It is the best way of influencing and persuading them from a psychological and also from a physiological perspective.

Whether you will be standing in front of them or communicating by other means (webinar, TV presentation, online conference call) the internet is an amazing resource to find out what is happening in their world.

YOUR MISSION, SHOULD YOU WISH TO ACCEPT IT, is to spend a portion of your week and if possible each day to:

> Research LinkedIn to find what others are saying about what is happening in your target market and comment on their posts.

> Write articles and posts on your topic to offer insights and value so that you are perceived as a thought leader.

> It is a fact that when you comment on subjects that are 'of the moment' in an article you will get somewhere between 60 – 80 views. When you write a succinct post with an appropriate photo or illustration the views rise to anything between 250 to over 3,000 views.

> In both of the above situations this means that your profile and observations extend far beyond your direct contacts.

> Research the websites of companies that you are targeting to find out what their Chairman and CEO are saying about their company and their aspiration for it.

Chapter 8

NETWORKING

-----❖-----

Maximising your time, your energy and the money you spend.

Scene 1 – A Party

"Look, over there, she's gorgeous". A blond with sultry blue eyes had just entered the room and was animatedly talking to her friend.

"Go on then, go over to her and ask her to dance" urged my pal David.

"I can't."

"Yes you can, go before anybody else does".

With great trepidation I crossed the room and with my heart pounding, my hands sweaty I tapped her on the shoulder and with the words almost catching in my throat I asked, "Would you like to dance"?

Turning slowly her beautiful eyes met mine, my Hank Marvin style glasses glinting in the dimmed light. She looked me up and down from my floral shirt to my white trousers and my winkle picker shoes. It was the sixties after all. "No, thanks," she said dismissively, and turned back to her friend to continue their chat. I knew they would be laughing at me as I walked away.

Scene 2 – At Home

"Mum! Mum! Mum!" – "Don't interrupt can't you see I'm talking?"

"But Mum, it's important."

"Dexter, stop it, it's rude to interrupt when people are talking."

Scene 3 – At School

"Moscow, if you haven't got anything worthwhile to add to the conversation best keep your mouth shut." (Mr Roach, my English teacher).

Don't Talk to Strangers

From very early on we are programmed not to break into conversations, fearful that by speaking up we may make a fool of ourselves or worst of all worried that we will be rejected.

Perhaps that's why so many of us find networking so daunting.

Over the years I have spent countless hours of my valuable time and a fortune in money attending a myriad of networking events all around the UK. They have been held in pubs, clubs, bars, hotels, restaurants and, increasingly, in impressive offices of bankers, accountants and lawyers.

I have sat at long tables at breakfast meetings. Joined round tables at luncheon clubs, stood around at speed networking (hate them) and open sessions where people wander from group to group drink or food in hand. I've joined delegates at symposiums, conferences, and evening seminars and listened to panel discussions followed by drinks and canapes.

I have even presented at an event in an Aston Martin showroom in Cheshire and a Ferrari showroom in Park Lane London.

Faced with all of these opportunities to meet people that might do business with you how do you determine what and where is best for you?

Let's explore how you can maximise your activities in these different environments and discover which strategies are the best to help you to win business and gain effective referrals.

I want to put words in your mouth, if you're not good at small talk, and offer a framework to create that short introduction, known as an 'elevator pitch' that identifies compelling reasons for someone to listen to what you have to say.

I want to enable you to break into seemingly closed groups and suggest ways to get away from bores and people that speak 'at you' so you can meet more interesting and relevant people.

Let me first explode a myth.

Networking is not a selling opportunity!

If that is a revelation then you have already missed some golden opportunities to make meaningful contacts.

Let me qualify this. It is not an opportunity to sell to the person in front of you. It is an opportunity to connect with individuals who may lead you to people who need your help, their clients and contacts.

Networking certainly is an opportunity to meet new people and start a relationship with them. It also gives you an opportunity to reconnect with those you may not have spoken to for some time.

Reconnection with people who already know you and what you do offers a great opportunity to update them on your activities. This may lead to referrals and, perhaps, even to doing business with them directly as there is already a relationship in place.

Let me explain further why, when you meet someone for the first time you should not try to sell to them.

Put yourself in their place. How many times have you been cornered at one of these events by someone who is only interested in pitching their business? They may have asked what you do, but actually all they want to do is get their selling message across regardless of whether it has any relevance for you.

It's an untargeted, scatter-gun approach that ends with them thrusting their business card into your hand and then asking for yours. It is annoying, insulting and achieves nothing.

The mantra I have been banging on about in the previous chapters is very relevant here; people hate being sold to. They love being consulted and have people showing sincere interest in them and what they do.

There is a major advantage here in firstly finding out about the other person. Why, because in doing so you immediately find out whether it is worthwhile spending time with them or whether you need to move on to the next person.

Now that we have established the best approach when engaging with people, let's look at some ground rules for effective networking.

Choose the Right Groups

The right groups for you need to be relevant to your business aspirations. If you're trying to meet senior executives at large corporates you won't meet many of them at local business breakfasts as they tend to be owner/managers of smaller businesses.

First find out what groups are available in your chosen area and explore the typical attendees. If you can't get this information, it may be worth attending one meeting to find out if they're a good fit for you.

Monthly Meetings

If you want to do business with C-suite executives, PLCs, top law firms, accountancy practices, insurance companies and high level professional firms, find the locations in your city where these individuals congregate.

Typically Chambers of Commerce, Institutes of Directors, Executive Networks and Leaders Clubs are where the level of individuals you would like to connect with meet.

These organisations usually get together every month and regularly have presentations by thought-leaders, influential individuals who are pre-eminent in their field of activity and experts who can offer insights into the industry sectors you are focused on.

Some networking clubs also meet monthly at lunchtimes or for breakfast and attendees are arranged around tables in cabaret style. There is an opportunity to present to your table what you do and circulate amongst other tables to network.

In addition, as a member you may even be invited to make a front of room presentation about your business of up to an hour.

The presentation frameworks you've explored in previous chapters can be used here.

The framework for table presentations is outlined in the next section.

Breakfast Meetings

If your business is one that sells products directly to consumers such as beauty preparations, health care, cleaning products or food etc., or you are an accountant, estate agent, local lawyer, charity, car mechanic, cleaner, offer I.T. support services, web design, printing etc., a weekly or fortnightly breakfast group could be an excellent place to generate business.

I advise you to join networks that have members that work with SMEs that can introduce you to their clients, customers and colleagues. You may even do business directly with the other members.

Here are some organisations you may want to research:
BOB Clubs https://www.bobclubs.com/club/country/uk
BRX http://www.brxnet.co.uk/
BNI https://www.bni.co.uk/
4Networking http://4networking.net/
There are also monthly lunches, often aimed at women, such as:
Women in Business Networking http://www.wibn.co.uk/
The Athena Network http://theathenanetwork.co.uk/

And there are many independent groups or smaller local networks too.

The key value in attending these meetings is that, over a period of time, strong relationships are built. Because the other members know, like and trust you they become your business ambassadors, referrers and connection makers.

This deep understanding of what you do is reinforced by the weekly opportunity you have of making a presentation to the group as a whole. A stand-up presentation that can be a two-minute conversation or a 'minute to win it' story.

The most effective are those that speak about what you have done in the previous week and how you have helped others.

This gives an insight of what you can do for their contacts and clients and makes asking for specific referrals easy. This is the key to your success in these clubs.

The added advantage of these associations is that many will give you the opportunity of speaking for 15 minutes or longer at some point in the year. Here you can go into greater detail about your company, its services and the testimonials you have received.

My advice is to grab these opportunities with open arms and put into practice your presentation skills.

TOP TIP

As a member of most of these groups you are expected to turn up every week. Some of them insist that, if you are not able to attend, you must send a representative or substitute.

As a member you are entitled to put yourself on the substitute list and can then be asked by a member in any other group to attend on their behalf.

This means that you will give their 1 or 2 minute presentation and also to do your own presentation. Your breakfast is paid for and you get the opportunity of attending groups and meeting people that you may not otherwise have been able to do. This widens your sphere of influence and opportunities for gaining further referrers.

Dislike working the room?

Unlike in the previous chapter where working the room is an essential element for gaining a direct understanding of your audience's needs, in networking situations many of us find approaching people 'on spec' daunting.

In truth, I also hate working the room. The concept of speaking to as many individuals as possible and getting their business cards and following up with emails goes against my ethos of creating meaningful relationships.

To address these concerns I would like to share with you some strategies that I have developed over the years for making these connections in a sophisticated way.

Body Language

In open networking situations where people are standing around with drink or food in hand and wander from group to group you may be reluctant to break into seemingly closed conversations.

Look at the body language of those in the group. Do some of them have their feet pointing out of the circle? This is a clear indication that they are trying to get away. Are their eyes glazing over or searching the room for a place to escape.

This is your opportunity to enter the circle and many will be grateful to you for intervening.

Positioning

There are to two locations in the room where people congregate and it's easy to start a conversation. By the bar or by the buffet. At some point during the event most people will visit these areas.

Propping up the bar in these circumstances is very acceptable.

Moving On

One of the most difficult situations in networking is how to move on from a person when you have realised that there is no value in continuing the conversation or they are boring the pants off you.

Here are a few strategies and suggested forms of words that enable you to move on seamlessly, without offending anyone.

> *"It's been great speaking to you. I don't want to take up any more of your time as we're both here to meet other interesting people so I'll leave you to connect with them".*

> *"Thanks for the chat, really appreciated understanding more about your activates, may I introduce you to ...?" At this point you take them over to someone else, introduce them and move on.*

> *"I've already taken up too much of your time, is there anybody I can introduce you to?"*

> *"Would you excuse me, I promised I would make contact with ...?"*

"I'm going to get a drink (or some food) would you excuse me?" You run the risk of them following you, but you can then engage in conversation with someone else at the bar or buffet.

TOP TIP

At most networking events you will be issued with a badge or asked to put your business cards in a clear badge. Clip these as high up on your clothing as possible and place it on the right.

When people shake hands with you the right-hand side is normally where their eyes naturally go so they see your name.

Two advantages here, when a person knows your name and can see what you do it makes for a more relaxed conversation. When you are reconnecting with someone you have met before it saves them the embarrassment of asking your name.

You may well feel it worthwhile having a badge made up specifically for networking purposes that has your name and company in bolder, larger type.

Not Good at Small Talk

Often, my clients tell me that they are not good at small talk and find it difficult to enter into conversation with people they don't know.

This is a tried and tested framework if you feel the same way. It is called the conversation stack and is attributed to Dale Carnegie training.

Firstly I would like to tell you a story and ask you to visualise the following:

> Imagine a **HOUSE ON A HILL** with a white picket fence running around it.
>
> You open the gate and walk up to the front door and there see a **BRASS NAME PLATE.**
>
> You walk into the front room and see a shelf and on the shelf are **FAMILY PHOTOGRAPHS.**
>
> You walk out into the garden and at the back of the garden is a **TALL OFFICE BLOCK.**
>
> Flying over the office block is an **AEROPLANE.**
>
> On one of the wings a **TENNIS RACQUET.**
>
> Above the aeroplane is a **LIGHT BULB.**

The purpose of creating these visual images and identifying the key words is to aid your recall of the stack with ease.

If you haven't already worked out the significance of these elements here's how this works:

HOUSE ON THE HILL – Where do you live, how did you get here?

BRASS NAME PLATE - I see your name is..., what do you do?

FAMILY PHOTOGRAPHS – Do you have a family/partner/kids?

TALL OFFICE BLOCK – Where do you work, what specifically do you do?

AEROPLANE – Are you going away on holiday this year? Have you already been away?

TENNIS RACQUET – Do you play sports, follow a team?

LIGHT BULB – Any other questions that occur to you.

In my experience there are 4 key rules to effective networking and developing strong relationships that may ultimately result in business.

Rapport

The dictionary defines rapport as 'a close and harmonious relationship in which the people or groups concerned understand each other's feelings or ideas and communicate well'.

It is essential to build rapport before speaking about business or how you might help each other. The golden rule that people buy people first is absolutely relevant here. Find common ground, opinions that resonate with each other, situations that you can agree on.

The key as always is to ask more questions. In doing so you create a deeper understanding of the other person. This leads to rapport because you are able to speak in terms of their interests.

Passion

If you are not passionate about what you do how can you create passion in others. As we have previously discussed this is shown in your demeanour and your sincere interest in the other person.

Trust

During the course of your conversation, stories are the best way of developing trust. A story demonstrates what you have achieved for others and how that may aid their client, customers or colleagues.

Elements of both the Four Cornerstones and the Incident – Action - Benefit frameworks can be used here. Remember always make them relevant to the person you are talking to and their occupation.

Integrity

How do you demonstrate integrity? It will come partly from the stories you tell and how you have kept your promises to other people.

There is a principle that we all should adhere to; 'We are judged not by the promises we make, but by the promises we keep.'

In networking terms this means that if you have said that we will make an introduction ensure that you do. If you have agreed to send some information, similarly do so.

Integrity for me is the foundation on which meaningful relationships are formed. It also ties in with one of Robert Cialdini's 6 principles of influence;

Reciprocity.

Keep your promises and others will feel obliged to help you.

You may have noticed that most of this chapter is focused on the other person and finding out about what they do.

The rationale behind this is, firstly, to make a judgment about whether it is worthwhile spending your precious time with this person and, secondly, gaining knowledge and understanding of what they do and may need so that you can target your offering.

The 30 Second Commercial.

This is a carefully thought-out, carefully crafted response to the question "What do you do?"

Accepting that I have counselled you always to find out about the other person and their activities, at some point in the conversation, you will have to (and want to) explain what you do.

Let's explore the concept of developing a 30-second commercial, also known as an 'elevator pitch'.

According to Wikipedia:

> *The concept of an 'elevator pitch' reflects the idea that it should be possible to deliver the summary in the timespan of an elevator ride, or approximately thirty seconds to two minutes. It is widely credited to Ilene Rosenzweig and Michael Caruso (while he was editor for Vanity Fair) for its origin.*
>
> *The term itself comes from a scenario of an accidental meeting with someone important in the elevator. If the conversation inside the elevator in those few seconds is interesting and value adding, the conversation will either continue after the elevator ride, or end in exchange of business cards or a scheduled meeting.*

It is essential that you make your response to that 'What do you do?' question impactful, relevant and compelling. It must contain information that engages the listener immediately and allows them to see what's in it for them.

It's common in networking, but it is also relevant in other circumstances where you need to get your message across fast.

The 30-second commercial should contain the following elements:

- Who you typically work with.

- In what industry or sector.

- Three situations that are not working for them and causing them worry and keeping them up at night. The key to the 30-second commercial proposition is to use phrases and pain words and identify negative experiences you know that they suffer in their specific industry.

- The commercial should end in an open question that requires a response from the person you are speaking to.

Here are some examples from organisations I have worked with:

Typically, I work with executives in the property industry.

Who are frustrated that they are not motivating their team effectively.

Or

Irritated that pitches are not gaining support from their investors

Or

Worried that the cost of their pitches are not winning the amount of business they require

I don't suppose that is happening in your industry or to people you know?

Typically I work with high net worth individuals and their P.A's who lease aircraft.

Who are frustrated that they are not gaining the level of service they require.

Or

They are irritated that they do not get the quality of aircraft they expect

Or

They are worried that the lack of quality reflects badly on them.

I don't suppose that is happening in your industry or to people you know.

Here is a blank for you to fill in with the appropriate 3 scenarios effecting the industries and the people you work with.

*Typically I work with (**WHO**) individuals in the (**INDUSTRY/SECTOR**).*

*Who are (**PAIN WORD**) that they are not (**APPROPRIATE NEGATIVE SITUATION**).*

Or

*They are (**PAIN WORD**) that they do not (**APPROPRIATE NEGATIVE SITUATION**).*

Or

*They are (**PAIN WORD**) that the (**APPROPRIATE NEGATIVE SITUATION**).*

I don't suppose that is happening in your industry or to people you know.

In any situation where you are seeking to understand the other person and finding out what is happening for them both personally and professionally there is a formula we need to adhere to.

It is called the 70% - 30% rule and is used by all the best sales people. To avoid confusion this is not Pareto's 80-20 rule but one known as The 70/30 Rule of Communication. This rule states that you should get the prospect to do 70% of the talking during a sales conversation and the sales person should only do 30% of the talking. This is a smart move in any conversation where you want to get the most positive results. Your 30% can be invested in asking deeper and more searching questions, having asked permission to do so.

This process can also be used when you are in a prospecting or face-to-face business pitching situation.

You will learn far more about your prospects fear, worries and pain when you ask searching question.

Next Steps

The key to successful networking is as follow-. If you have exchanged business cards and had a productive conversation with some interesting people and you feel that you could create some mutually beneficial referrals, make contact with them within 48 hours.

In this situation an email is certainly acceptable. Here is a suggested template:

Dear...,

It was great meeting you at ... and I really enjoyed our conversation and hope you did too.

Perhaps we could get together for a coffee to explore how we might help each other and see what connections we can make.

Please give me a ring on 07973 635670 if you feel it would be useful.

Warm regards,

Alternatively, if you have really got on well, why not ask if they would like to arrange a date for coffee there and then. Be sure to send then a formal diary invitation. Confirm the arrangement a day or so before the actual appointment. People do have second thoughts or important business demands need to take precedence.

The final element of follow-up is to connect with them on LinkedIn. In this way you can explore their contacts and identify specific individuals or companies that you would like referrals into when you have your follow-up meeting.

Here is another template you might find useful:

Dear .....,

It was great meeting you at ....

If you feel it of value I'd like to add you to my professional network.

Have a look at my contacts and let me know who interests you.

Warm regards,

Dexter

Exercise 8 – Develop Your Own 30 Second Commercial

Create 30-second commercials for each sector or for the individuals you come into contact with.

What are three specific elements that you know are causing them worry?

Compile a list of pain words and pain situations that you can use when the appropriate situation arises.

Chapter 9

FURTHER THOUGHTS

-----◆----

THE 4 E's FULLY EXPLAINED - ENGAGE - ENLIGHTEN - ENTERTAIN – EXCITE

I was working with one of the largest property development and investment companies in the UK and they were arranging an away day for the executive finance team. The intention was to explain the direction the company was taking.

The instructions were to make the day interactive, informative and fun, allowing for the fact that a number of the topics were very dry, heavy (as they had to cover all the regulatory issues) and complex.

One particular person was asked to outline his role as a treasury professional, dealing with managing the money and financial risks in the business. He was to speak on economic factors, such as interest rate rises, changes in regulations and volatile foreign exchange rates. All intense and multi-faceted subjects.

Having been invited to the stage by one of his colleagues he made his way to the front of the room to the theme from Only Fools and Horses. For those of you who have never seen this TV series, it's about a fast-talking market trader living in South London who, in order to try to get rich, dabbles in black market trading. The absolute opposite of the person who was about to speak and the subject he was about to speak on.

He was greeted with applause and good humoured laughter and using this unique twist on his role proceeded to explain the similarities between Del-Boy Trotter, the main character in the show, and his duties negotiating the best finance deals for the company.

The feedback from his colleagues was that, for the first time, they understood exactly what he did and how important it was for the business.

Remember the four Strategic Pillars of every presentation – the 4 E's? This is a brilliant example of one of them (I'll let you guess which one). Let's explore this process in greater depth.

Engage

I've emphasised the importance of engagement repeatedly and I just want to give you a final reminder of the golden rules:

- The 30-second impactful opening.
- The 7-10 minute rule of pressing the attention reset button.
- Pattern Interrupts – Doing something different and unexpected.
- Use a prop or other device to reengage.

The Case for Engagement

You know the importance of maintaining eye contact with your audience and how using PowerPoint breaks this connection. It is also true when you are continually reading from your slides or, worse still, reading directly from your notes. This not only breaks the connection between you and your audience, but also sends a message that you don't know your material or someone else has prepared it for you.

Recently I attended a forum to discuss the effects of the latest political pronouncements on the insurance sector. The company hosting the event is a major player in this area and the speaker representing the company was very knowledgeable and personable.

His talk was divided into two parts. The first was a slide presentation showing the credibility of his organisation in terms of longevity, some facts and figures showing its standing in the sector and its worldwide reach.

The information on the slides was bullet pointed, almost all text, difficult to read, self-congratulatory and, frankly, boring. What was worse, the presenter read the information word-for-word off the screen.

Clearly, he had been told that he had to use these slides and it was obvious that they had been prepared *for* him, rather than *by* him.

This compared dramatically to the second half of his presentation which was energetic, engaging, relevant and related to the fears and concerns we all have about political intervention.

The animated way he presented the second element of his talk demonstrated that this subject was both close to his heart. Occasionally he glanced down at his notes, but in the main he kept eye contact with us.

His whole demeanour was completely changed from the opening slide section to the conversational style of the second section. You could see him physically drop his shoulders, exhale and relax into this part of his talk.

After the presentation I congratulated him on the talk, but suggested that the company credibility element of his presentation would have had greater impact if he had told us not what the company does, but had given us specific illustrations of what the company does for its clients.

There are a number of key lessons to be learnt here:

- **Know your material** – reading off the slides can damage your credibility.

- **Make it relevant to the audience** – starting with a pitch alienates your audience.

- **Tell stories** rather than show heavily text-filled slides – tell me what you do for your clients, not just what you do.

- **Maintain passion throughout** all elements of the presentation.

- **Keep eye contact with the audience –** don't read the slides or your notes

- **Refer to your notes only to confirm where you are in the presentation.**

Enlighten

There are three main reasons why people read a book, listen to a presentation or go to a seminar:

TO GAIN INFORMATION or acquire a nugget of insight that is valuable to them or their organisation. The ability to report back on or teach others in their company about something validates them spending their and their company's valuable time and money.

TO GAIN CONFIRMATION that what they are doing is right and that they should keep on doing it. There is great comfort knowing that what you believe and do is valid with supporting evidence.

It is also provides a benchmark of success and everybody, regardless of their position in a company, seeks positive endorsement for their activities.

F.O.M.O. (**Fear Of Missing Out) –** This is the greatest driver and motivation for learning something new. The concern that your competitors are doing something that you are not, that they are stealing a march on you in your market place and that you may be losing out to them is a powerful driver.

PAIN is a compelling reason to get people to change, do something differently and think in a different way.

Entertain

Even in a situation where the topic you are speaking on is weighty, important and, maybe, controversial you still have to entertain.

As before this doesn't mean you have to sing and dance, tell jokes or juggle in front of your audience. Think what you can do to get your key points across with impact so that people remember them and are motivated to take action.

Did you guess that this was the E that our away day financial speaker got right on target?

Excite

If you're not passionate about what you do, how can you make others passionate about it?

This may appear obvious, but how many of us have seen presentations where the presenter was not fully engaged with their topic and it came across as lacklustre and unconvincing?

The phrase that comes to mind is "If you are really excited about what you're saying – tell your face." In other words let your feelings show, it helps your audience to engage emotionally.

The Angel with Detachable Wings

I was working at QVC during the run up to Christmas selling various products and decorations. On this occasion I was asked to sell a fibre optic angel standing some three feet tall with wings that could be removed for ease of storage.

In truth, I was not personally enamoured by the effigy, so how could I sell this with passion and excitement?

I considered what the best way I could present it was and this is how the sell went.

"Many people believe in Guardian Angels, that they are being looked after by loved ones and it is part of their faith".

"At this time of year it is comforting to feel that there may be someone looking out for us and this beautiful colourful figurine is the embodiment of that belief."

We had 50 to sell at £35 each and in 4 minutes we sold out. Approaching £450 per minute? Not bad.

The lesson here is that, if you are not sold yourself, put yourself in your audience's shoes. See it from their perspective, understand what is happening in their world and be excited for them.

A warning though: not everybody will be impressed, especially friends.

This is a true story I tell in my workshops.

I returned home from the studio at 3 in the morning as the last show had gone out live at 2 am. I noticed the light on the answer machine was flashing.

I picked up the receiver pressed the button to hear "Dex (splutter, guffaw, uncontrolled laughter) Angel – pause – "Detachable wings" – more laughter and incomprehensible words, further pause, "Here's Colin".

Then in a more measured tone, "Dex? If an Angel has detachable wings", pause for effect, "How the F… can it fly?" The message ended amid more laughter.

Some people have no soul.

Mind Mapping

I mentioned Mind Mapping briefly in Chapter 4, let's explore this in greater depth – it's a very useful tool.

It is a method that enables you to recall your presentation, its order and how to deliver it without referring to your notes. Having laboured the point about the importance of remembering your presentation this is a process to do it.

How do you recall the order, remember the content, when to pause for effect and use pattern interrupts and attention reset buttons to maintain the audience's attention?

You can learn it word for word and recite it like a poem by heart. The danger here is that it may lack spontaneity, seem over-rehearsed and the delivery then becomes wooden and lacking passion.

Mind mapping is a process that taps into the way the brain 'sees' information using pictorial diagrams, visualisation and word associations. It is a graphical representation of ideas or topics using connecting lines each with a single word or image on each line.

Although it may seem random when viewed on the page it mirrors the brains own capacity to make logical connections.

Mind maps are used to visualise, organize, and classify ideas, making them perfect for study aids, organizing information, problem solving, making decisions and writing presentations.

Tony Buzan the originator of Mind Maps defines the following 10 rules for their creation:-

http://bit.do/DM-MM

Start in the centre with an image of the topic, using at least 3 colours.

Use images, symbols, codes, and dimensions throughout your mind map.

Select key words and print using upper or lower-case letters.

Each word/image is best alone and sitting on its own line.

The lines should be connected, starting from the central image. The lines become thinner as they radiate out from the centre.

Make the lines the same length as the word/image they support.

Use multiple colours throughout the Mind Map, for visual stimulation and also for encoding or grouping.

Develop your own personal style of Mind Mapping.

Use emphasis and show associations in your Mind Map.

Keep the mind map clear by using radial hierarchy or outlines to embrace your branches.

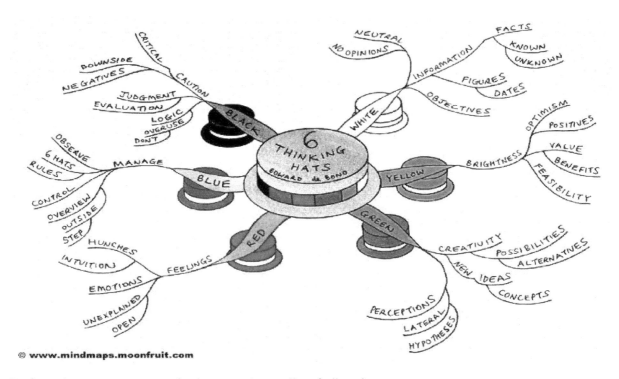

© www.mindmaps.moonfruit.com

Before I prepare my mind maps I use the following process.

Write out my presentation in full

Chunk it down into paragraphs

Define a key sentence that is the essence of the paragraph

Choose a word that sparks the memory of the paragraph

Enter those words on the developing Mind Map.

Re-draw the Mind Map to ensure the connected thoughts make sense and flow.

Case Study

How I created an hour-long presentation to motivate non-sales people to sell

For a period of time I worked in the retirement homes industry. My role was to set up an in-house estate agency to help the property owners and their relatives to sell their flats and houses, instead of having to use outside estate agents.

I had taken up this position after three others had failed to achieve the projected targets.

The key was to engage with and enrol the help of the House Managers, whose main duty was to look after the daily welfare of the residents and be there in emergencies. Their role was NOT to be an estate agent.

It was, however, essential that they became part of the process. They held waiting lists for people who wanted to purchase on the sites and had information on the availability of the properties.

The sites were scattered throughout the UK and my first objective was to develop a feeling of trust with the Managers. That would be no easy task as to-date they had experienced a virtual revolving door of Sales Directors.

My priorities would be to convince them that I had the necessary abilities to follow through on the promises I would make to them. They needed to TRUST me to support them at any time during the sales process and believe that I would make myself available to the residents where necessary.

This meant attending resident's association meetings, AGMs and social events. Although outside my remit as Sales Director it was very important to convince the residents that I was a safe pair of hands and that I could achieve market value for their property.

When I first took over the role as Sales Director I visited the sites all over the country and addressed audiences of up to 30 Managers. This is where a Mind Map helped me immensely. I prepared a single page map of my presentation that would be about an hour in length.

The essence of the presentation was to show the Managers that I fully understood, not only the problems of dealing with demanding older people, but the double challenge of them also being demanding residents. Many of these people although retired, had held executive positions or had come from a business background. They expected a high level of service and to be kept fully informed.

The Mind Map of my talk for the Managers was developed using **the Four Cornerstones of a Presentation** process:

My personal credibility was demonstrated by the stories I told about running my own estate agencies. I also gave humorous examples about the trials and tribulations of having an elderly Mother and Mother-in-Law. People like people who are like them and understand them.

Company credibility – Identifying the major property organisations I had worked with and what I had done for them.

3-4 key facts:

- The process I would employ to ensure the smooth running of the transactions
- The solicitor and outside agency contact I would maintain
- The chase up procedures I would utilise.

All to take the burden from the Managers of overseeing the transactions and reporting to the residents and their relatives.

What's in it for them?

- Financial incentives, earned for making introductions or gaining instructions on a property.
- My availability to sort out problems.
- Attending meetings and resolving other non-property related problems.

The same style of presentation was also made to the residents to engage with them and to engender their trust.

I revised my presentation so that I knew the running order and overall content. I did not rehearse it word for word, in this way I could make it fresh, deliver it with confidence and authority and without referring to my notes.

It also meant that when asked questions, as I often was, I had the confidence to know that I would not lose my train of thought and could easily pick up where I had left off.

In the first year of my involvement we increased turnover by 200%.

I was regularly invited to celebrate resident's birthdays, anniversaries and many other celebrations.

TOP TIP

If at any time you do lose your place and absolutely have to refer to your notes, try this:

"I would just like to check my notes to ensure that I have not missed anything important. I want to give you as much relevant information as I can?"

Pick up your notes, check and carry on.

The perception is that you are thinking about their needs rather than yours.

THE EPILOGUE

So, that's the **MOSCOW Method**.

In this book I have attempted to give you the essential elements of preparing a business winning presentation. Frameworks that, if adhered to, will enable you to persuade and influence your team members and executive. But if your content is not compelling and you are not able to develop a reasoned, easy-to-follow argument that others will buy into then all is for nothing.

I am not able to create the specifics of your presentation. What I hope I have done is to fulfil the promise I made to you at the beginning of this book give you some tried and tested concepts that ensures your talk flows and your audience is prepared to listen to your proposition.

To walk you through processes and methodologies that will enable you to prepare, construct and deliver business winning pitches.

Use these tools and techniques to make presentations so that your audience of one or many buy what you're selling, whether that's a product, a service or an idea.

Remember to use words and phrases and tell stories that are compelling and ensure that your audience takes the action you desire them to take.

The key to making all this work is the realisation that nothing can be achieved if you don't take the necessary ACTION to bring the ideas discussed to life. To follow the principles and use the TOP TIPS to showcase your knowledge, experience and passion.

It has been said that the only way to ensure that new information becomes part of you and your thinking is to practise, practise, practise. Because PRACTICE MAKES PERFECT.

The reality is that nothing is perfect, because perfection is only for the gods. Strive not for perfection, strive for excellence. Focus on the journey not on the destination.

In a sporting context, if your thinking centres on lifting the trophy, receiving the cheque and gaining the adoration of the crowd you will fail. Yes, it is essential that you have a compelling objective, a target, a great big hairy goal to achieve, but focus on winning the next point, scoring the next try, running the next mile.

My son recently completed his first London Marathon. His training was based on running longer and longer distances and over a period of 12 months. He built his stamina, his experience and understanding of what it takes to achieve his objective.

Sure, his ultimate goal was to complete the 26 miles and 385 yards in a realistic time, but when he actually ran the race to think in terms of the overall distance was daunting. His focus was on running the next mile and then the next and then the next until the finish line was in sight.

It was the crowd that buoyed him up, the cheers and chants of his name that carried him on through 'the wall' and beyond.

It is the same for us gain the support of your family and colleagues. Try out new ideas and ask them for their opinion on what you are doing.

Make your mantra PRACTICE MAKES **PERMANENT**.

When you take every opportunity to try the ideas you've explored here the process drops away and they form part of you and you become **Authentic**, have **Authority** and are **Accomplished**.

Look back at the key learning ideas, create your own stories or borrow them from your friends and colleagues. Re-read this book and if you have not already done so make notes, highlight paragraphs and carry out the instructions suggested.

There is a whole world of opportunities out there to make your most cherished dreams a reality.

We live in an age where you can develop a portfolio of occupations. Where you can have multiple careers and jobs that satisfy your heart's desire. Where, if you have the right determination and a fire in your belly you can achieve amazing success.

Napoleon Hill, American self-help author, said "Most great people have attained their greatest success just one step beyond their greatest failure."

In the words of the Traditional Gaelic Blessing:

May the road rise up to meet you.

May the wind be always at your back.

May the sun shine warm upon your face;

the rains fall soft upon your fields until we meet again,

Exercise 9 – Create Your Perfect Day – Visualisation

Every day for the next couple of weeks, get out of bed half an hour earlier than you normally do, find yourself a quiet spot and follow this process. It will take from 15–30 minutes, depending on the complexity of the situation you are going to address.

- Get yourself comfortable with your feet firmly on the floor and close your eyes.

- Take a deep breath in through your nose and exhale through your mouth.

- Take another deep breath in through your nose and exhale through your mouth.

- Take a third deep breath in through your nose and exhale through your mouth.

- Think about what appointments you have today, what tasks you need to perform, who you are due to be meeting with.

- Focus on how your body feels. What is giving you cause for concern or fear?

- Visualise yourself having the conversation, in the location, making the pitch or presentation.

- Run these interactions like a video in your head and see the successful outcome of these situations.

- Note any hesitation or areas of dispute and imagine how these can be resolved.

- See people agreeing to your propositions, pitches, ideas and services.

- Hear the conversation, see the locations, and make the colours bright, the sounds positive and supportive. Feel in your body the sense of pride and satisfaction for a job well done.

- Open your eyes and recall the positive feeling that suffuses every part of your being.

> *Before you can influence others you have to influence yourself.*

Acknowledgments

To Clive Thompson and David Pickering who generously allowed me to take all of the Dale Carnegie courses and coached me through my certification to become a Trained Dale Carnegie Trainer.

Marcus Cauchi of the Sandler Sales Institute for his unorthodox training methods in the Presidents' Club that enabled me to gain a deeper understanding of the psychology of selling, the motivation of why people buy and how to influence and persuade them to take the action we desire them to take.

QVC The Shopping Channel who, for 16 joyous years, gave me the opportunity to sell a myriad of products for major organisations on TV and coach and train guest presenters to excel at the art of 'selling on telly'. In effect selling to an invisible audience.

Steve Freedman whose sage counselling and gentle cajoling enabled me to do something that I had talked about for years, but never had the courage to sit down and do – write this book.

To my son Alex, who by recording our conversations, helped me to understand what my expertise is so that it could help others.

The Author

Dexter's grey hairs, what's left of them, have been gained through working and coaching at the highest level in the Finance, Property, Advertising, Sales, and Entertainment industries.

His associations with Reed International, the Dale Carnegie organisation, The Sandler Sales Institute and his live appearances, presenting on QVC The Shopping Channel, informs his unique approach to corporate communication, selling ideas and influencing skills.

As a keynote speaker and business coach, those working 1-2-1 with him and attending his presentations and sales courses have gained heightened communication abilities, new insights and increased confidence in selling, themselves and their business proposition.

As Managing Director of Audience Dynamics and a TV personality he specialises in coaching people to achieve communication excellence. He also conducts *Influencing Excellence* and *Master Influencing Excellence* seminars.

These interactive workshops focus on consultative and personal sales skills in all aspects of that term, He has created a number of highly effective training models including The 9 steps to Sales P.O.T.E.N.T.I.A.L., a tried and tested system that ensures to put you in control of the sales process, and *How to sell to an invisible audience* using a unique system – The 7 keys to P.E.R.F.E.C.T. communication – a process to win more business.

He has also developed *How to Sell at a Seminar without Selling* using the MOSCOW method, which enables seminar speakers to leverage their presentations.

Graduates of these interventions are empowered to persuade, engage and develop instant rapport with diverse audiences. This results in effective communication, buy-in from colleagues, more sales and greater brand recognition.

References

P11   Richard Branson

P12, 53   David Sandler, The Sandler Sales Institute

P13   Donald Trump

P13   Nigel Farage

P13   Simon Cowell

P13   Tony Blair

P14, 20   Dr Joseph Lowery

P20, 31   Dale Carnegie

P31   Warren Buffett

P34   Maya Angelou, American poet and civil rights activist

P35   Julian Ballantyne

P35   Mike Nichols, film director

P36   Daniel Kadish PhD, Psychologist, New York

P36   Aymeric Guillot PhD, Professor at the Centre of Research & Innovation in Sport. University Claude Bernard Lyon, France.

P37   Tom Seabourne, PhD. Author of *The Complete Idiot's Guide to Quick Total Body Workouts*

P38   Michael Gervais, PhD. Performance psychologist, Los Angeles

P38   Tammy Miller, Speech Coach, State College, Pennsylvania

P38   Kay Porter PhD, Sports Psychology consultant, author of *The Mental Athlete*

P41   Richard Bandler, inventor of NLP

P41   Milton H Erickson, psychiatrist and psychologist specialising in medical hypnosis and family therapy.

Also Available from Parvus Magna Press

The Little Black Book for Entrepreneurs – Matthew Black

The Little Black book for entrepreneurs is a workbook for those with business ideas to help them get their business from the back of a napkin to the stock exchange.

Full of worksheets and practical advice that can be easily implemented and tracked.

Everything from finance to networking and sales and marketing is covered in this workbook.

Matthew is known as the Outback Entrepreneur and is an established start-up business coach.

http://bit.do/DMMB
ISBN: 978-1-910372-04-3

£9.99

Every business has someone who has to fill the role of the Finance Director, whether that is the person who runs the business as Managing Director or a dedicated finance professional.

In this seminary work on the role of the Finance Director—Chairman of the Association of Finance and Risk Liam Wall investigates the advantages of a properly trained finance director and what that will mean to your business environment.

A finance professional should be a critical component of growing your business and taking it to the next level.

http://bit.do/DMFDA
£9.99

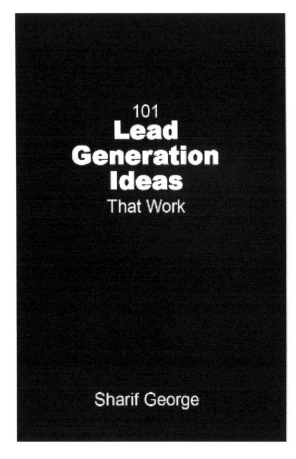

The So you started running your own small business but you quickly come to the realisation that you needed a bit more than just the ability to deliver your services to clients.

One of the biggest challenges for us is getting leads into the business. We were trained as IT consultants, Accountants, Lawyers, Coaches and Artisans.

We were not trained into how to sell and in the early part of our businesses life it can be difficult to find the cash to bring in professional help.

This book helps bridge the gap, with two bonus sections on online lead management and search engines.

Start Generating leads without spending a fortune.

ISBN: 978-1-910372-02-9 eBook
ISBN: 978-1-910372-03-6 Paperback
http://bit.do/DM101
£9.99

Printed in Great Britain
by Amazon